BRITISH WRITERS AND THEIR WORK: NO. 3

General Editor

T. O. Beachcroft

Editor of the American Edition

J. W. Robinson

VIRGINIA WOOLF

by Bernard Blackstone

E. M. FORSTER

by Rex Warner

KATHERINE MANSFIELD

by Ian A. Gordon

UNIVERSITY OF NEBRASKA PRESS · LINCOLN

Virginia Woolf by Bernard Blackstone, *Katherine Mansfield* by Ian A.
Gordon, and *E. M. Forster* by Rex Warner originally appeared separately
in pamphlet form, published by Longmans, Green & Co. for The British
Council and the National Book League [of Great Britain]. The Bison
Book edition is published by arrangement with The British Council.

Manufactured in the United States of America

PREFACE

BRITISH WRITERS AND THEIR WORK is addressed to the student who wants a general introduction to a particular writer or group of writers, and also to the more advanced student and to the lover of literature who enjoy fresh, thoughtful literary criticism. Each volume includes essays on from two to six writers, the series as a whole being planned to consider British men of letters from the fourteenth century to the present day. The essays in most instances combine the biography of a writer with a critical appreciation of his work. Many of the contributors are themselves well-known English authors and critics.

The essays originally were published separately for The British Council under the titles listed on the copyright page. They are reprinted in the American edition with minor corrections.

It is hoped that not only will the essays prove useful and stimulating, but that the select bibliographies will make each volume a convenient, portable reference work. While the arrangement will vary somewhat from volume to volume, each essay usually is followed by a full list of the first editions of the writer's works (provided as a complement to the account in the essay); a list of collected editions, modern reprints, and student editions; a list of bibliographies and reference works; and a list of critical and biographical studies (including both standard works and other works found especially useful by the author of the essay). Each volume ordinarily concludes with a list of general works. The select bibliographies, compiled by the editor of the American edition, are based largely on the bibliographies originally published with the essays.

J. W. R.

CONTENTS

VIRGINIA WOOLF

by Bernard Blackstone

VIRGINIA WOOLF

¶Virginia Woolf, daughter of Sir Leslie Stephen and wife of Leonard Woolf, was born in 1882 and died in 1941.

VIRGINIA WOOLF

I

THE WRITER AND THE AGE

IN the maelstrom of 'movements' that make up the literature of our time and country, we may distinguish two
separate and contrary directions. There is the centrifugal
and there is the centripetal current. There is the literature of
action—'in the destructive element immerse'; there is the
literature of recollection—'be still and know'. One current
goes with the age; the other opposes it. Yet both are integral
to our time, the maelstrom could not exist without them.

That double position accepted, there is no difficulty in
pointing out the major figures. On the one hand, Joyce,
Lawrence, and the novel of violence; on the other, Forster,
Myers, Virginia Woolf. In poetry, similar distinctions can
be made. There are political overtones, more audible perhaps in the thirties than today. Stretching a few points, we
can sniff religious odours: here, incense and guttering
candles, there, dusty hassocks and the cold stone of college
chapels. The one school, floating in a refined air of mystical
agnosticism, looks askance on the sex-cum-blasphemy of the
other.

If we ask ourselves in what consists the specific modernity
of modern literature, either of the left or the right (as I shall
call the two 'currents', without political implication), we
may find the answer far to seek. Is modern literature everything in 'serious' prose and verse written after a particular
date, say 1918? Hardly that; for it is notorious that a good
deal of highly respected work done since that date might
well have been written, as far as its concern with present-day
living goes or as far as it shows an awareness of contemporary technique, at any point in the past half century.
Moreover, a considerable amount of work which does
display this awareness was written well before 1918—much

of the verse of Yeats and Hopkins, most of Forster's prose.
We cannot leave this out of account, or we may get a false
perspective.

If modernity is not a matter of chronology, what is it?
Well, of course chronology comes into the picture. The
writer must deal with the events of his time; but, if he is a
good writer, in his hands they don't stay events, they
become experiences. Such a writer is not a mere reporter;
he is aware of the significance of what is happening in his
age, able to compass the broad pattern woven of separate
events. The journalist cannot see the wood for the trees;
the artist grasps the meaning behind phenomena. He is
something of a philosopher, a seer, as well as a technician.
But the technique comes in too. New wine won't go into
old bottles. New ideas, new ways of experience, shatter the
old forms. Inevitably, originality of thought and spontaneity
of emotion create fresh designs, strange music, new rhythms.
With some writers, like James Joyce, they even create a new
vocabulary. Indeed, if we find a poet (to evidence the
simpler art) using the old forms, the sonnet, the rondeau,
blank verse, and so on, we may be suspicious of him—as
suspicious as if we caught him aping the idiom of Milton
or Chaucer.

That is the first essential in the modern writer, I think:
awareness of what is new and important, and adequate
technical response to that awareness. Later we shall see that
there is a second 'note' of good writing, which I shall call
proportion. But for the moment let us focus on this aspect,
since it provides a useful introduction to our theme in this
essay. Virginia Woolf is commonly held to be a 'difficult'
writer, which means that she didn't use a conventional
technique or seek to arouse stock responses in her readers.
She was aiming at something new, and we may safely say
that she achieved it. What was this something new?

To answer this question fully would entail a discussion of
the position of the English novel at the time when Virginia
Woolf began to write—around, that is to say, 1915. But I

have already had something to say about this in an earlier
and lengthier study of her work; and in an essay as brief as
the present one there is no room for any but positive findings.
I would like to make this, not a conducted tour, but a series
of flashes focused now on one, now on another aspect of her
art. What has she new to offer the reader? What dimension
of understanding? What peculiar insights? In discussing
these questions we may find that we are also, in effect,
probing into some of the general conditions of the modern
novel; for it is futile to consider any writer otherwise than
within the context of his time. In the case of Virginia
Woolf, we shall find especially profitable the distinction,
which I made first of all, between the two currents of the
contemporary maelstrom.

The first characteristic of Virginia Woolf's that strikes me
is her understanding of human insufficiency. There are
affinities here, of course, with the left—with existentialism
and the novel of violence; but where the existentialists give
up in despair and the Lawrences and Greenes seek their
panacea in action—that is, in the movement away from the
still centre—Virginia Woolf works consistently inwards,
away from the world of events. Let us begin with an example
from her last novel, *Between the Acts* (1941). Here we have a
positive statement, that is, a presentation of a moment of
sufficiency: but we are shown how that moment can exist
only under certain special conditions: in the mind of a
child rather than an adult, in the absence of distraction, and
exposed to the threat of instant destruction.

> Amy was saying something about a feller when Mabel, with her
> hand on the pram, turned sharply, her sweet swallowed. 'Leave off
> grubbing,' she said sharply. 'Come along, George.'
> The little boy had lagged and was grouting in the grass. Then the
> baby, Caro, thrust her fist over the coverlet and the furry bear was
> jerked overboard. Amy had to stoop. George grubbed. The
> flower blazed between the angles of the roots. Membrane after
> membrane was torn. It blazed a soft yellow, a lambent light under
> a film of velvet, it filled the caverns behind the eyes with light. All

that inner darkness became a hall, leaf smelling, earth smelling of
yellow light. And the tree was beyond the flower; the grass, the
flower and the tree were entire. Down on his knees grubbing he held
the flower complete. Then there was a roar and a hot breath and a
stream of coarse grey hair rushed between him and the flower. Up
he leapt, toppling in his fright, and saw coming towards him a
terrible peaked eyeless monster moving on legs, brandishing arms.

Little George's moment of sufficiency is flanked by two
insufficiencies: the nursemaids with their talk of 'fellers'
and their sweets, the old man with his Afghan hound and
the need to impose himself on his grandson. The vision
which consists in a perfect observation of and identification
with that which *is* (in this case the flower, roots, and soil at
the foot of a tree) is broken by the intrusion of an adult
world. This is the final example in Mrs. Woolf's work of a
repeated pattern. Let us note in passing that there is no
condemnation of the nursemaids for being stupid or of
Bart for being tyrannical: things are what they are, and we
have moved out of the moral, discriminating world of
Dickens and Thackeray. We might call this absence of
judgement a note of modernity, and indeed of maturity, for
Virginia Woolf did not display it from the outset. Her
early work, like Forster's, offers value-judgements, particularly in situations directed against organized religion and its
ministers. There is, it is true, a survival of this in the clergyman of *Between the Acts*, but a balance is preserved with
the sympathetic portrait of Lucy fingering her crucifix.

Yet Lucy, however sympathetically drawn, is plainly not
a self-sufficient person. She fingers her crucifix, she relies
on God. Let us, with George's experience in mind, watch
her cutting a loaf of bread.

Why's stale bread, she mused, easier to cut than fresh? And so
skipped, sidelong, from yeast to alcohol; so to fermentation; so to
inebriation; so to Bacchus; and lay under purple lamps in a vineyard
in Italy, as she had done, often.

We see what is happening. George perceives; Lucy muses.
George experiences; Lucy reacts. The bread is there, but she
does not *see* it. Her thoughts move in a chain; they are slung
on the string of memory. Information, morality, nostalgia,
all are there, all the debris which chokes the immediate and
masks the strange. George's mind is a cavern filled with
yellow light, smelling of earth, empty. He labels nothing,
moves on to nothing. He experiences that bliss. Lucy, in the
same situation, would be naming everything she saw and
relating it to past or future: 'Ah, a worm, there goes a beetle,
horrid thing, I must do something about these weeds, how
stony this soil is. . . .' The screen of concepts would be set
between her and reality.

And thus the uniqueness, the joy of the moment, escapes
her. As, indeed, Virginia Woolf shows it escaping so many
of her characters. Here is Mrs. Ramsay in *To the Lighthouse*,
sensing much that is true and good; but she verbalizes it:

> When life sank down for a moment, the range of experience
> seemed limitless. And to everybody there was always this sense of
> unlimited resources, she supposed; one after another, she, Lily,
> Augustus Carmichael, must feel, our apparitions, the things you
> know us by, are simply childish. Beneath it is all dark, it is all
> spreading, it is unfathomably deep; but now and again we rise to the
> surface and that is what you see us by.

Words fix her experience. Of course Virginia Woolf knows
the danger. Her art, in its development, aims at finding a
way out. The very 'stream-of-consciousness' technique
which we see at work in Lucy's interior monologue above,
and which Mrs. Woolf derived from Sterne and Proust, is
a means at least of bringing the evil to the surface, of
demonstrating how much we are bound in our mental
processes by memories, reactions, obsessions. But need the
writer also be bound in his art? That, for her, is the question.
And so we find her experimenting with technique. Can
words, can phrases, can the very structure of the novel be
stripped of their conventional trappings, made to evoke

other than stock responses? Can the reader be induced to
expect something different, or, if not to expect, at least to
accept it? Is it possible, above all, to emulate the technique
of the painter (we remember Virginia Woolf's interest in the
post-Impressionists) and say, 'There is what I saw—that is
how the thing you call a rose, a jam-jar, or a boat appeared
to me, then, at that moment, under those conditions of light
inner and outer'? Can the novel present, as the pictures can,
the thusness of each object as it exists in relationship to blue
sky, yellow sand, or striped table-cloth?

Let us note how curiously the theme of insufficiency is
again asserting itself—this time in the dubious relationship
of author and reader. It is the reader, you or I, who now
turns back from the immediate experience offered to him
by the novelist. The writer comes bearing gifts and is
greeted by a 'Timeo Danaos!' I offer you, says the novelist,
a new slant on life, the fresh perception that I have achieved;
I doubt if you have been given anything quite like it before.
I don't want your new perception, replies the reader, I
want Tarzan, or Forsyte, or the mixture as before of
Catholicism-and-violence. Go away and leave me in peace.
I don't want reality. It bores me and frightens me. In any
case, I don't understand you. I can't follow what you are
saying.

The reader cannot follow what the writer is saying because
she is trying to say it in a different way. Virginia Woolf
was, from first to last, intensely conscious of making a
different thing out of the novel. The *genre* had been
developed and exploited by men; but she was a woman,
and she was sure that a woman novelist had to create her own
form. Jane Austen had done it; but the Brontës and George
Eliot had stuck too close to the old masculine pattern. The
feminine mind, the feminine sensibility, cannot profitably
imitate the masculine. A woman novelist has something new
to bring. And so Virginia Woolf experiments ceaselessly in
new forms, fresh techniques, always trying to get nearer to
an integral expression of life. For truth—her great devotion

—is valid here as well as in the realm of ideas, in how a thing is said as well as in what is said. The form of the conventional, commercial novel is not *true*; it is stereotyped, deals only with certain detached aspects of living (which it exaggerates and distorts) glued together by the crude devices of set descriptions, coincidences, catastrophes, transition passages of mere padding. And all moves on the surface. How, thought Virginia Woolf, how could she find a form that would convey the movement of things under the surface—the free play of thought, emotion, insight?

She learned, of course, from others. Mostly from her contemporaries, from Proust and Joyce and Dorothy Richardson; but also from the older masters in whose work she discerned the same experimental quality, the same focusing on an interior world. There was Sterne, for instance, with his technique of disintegration, his flouting of the time sense and of the connecting link; there was Montaigne, with his delicately poised self-revelation, his irony; there were also the great Russians. In her first novels we feel rather strongly the influence of E. M. Forster. Indeed, these novels are not experimental in form; they are occupied more, after the Forster pattern, in probing the niceties of human relationships. She wants to find out what themes the novel should deal with, what kind of characters she herself is best fitted to present. *The Voyage Out* (1915) is a fairly straightforward narrative of a young girl, Rachel Vinrace, who is thrust suddenly out of a backwater into the whirl of life, falls in love, and dies. *Night and Day* (1919), is about another young girl, Katharine Hilberry, more self-possessed, more mature, who wonders whether falling in love and marrying may not be a matter of quitting life for a backwater. But in her next novel, *Jacob's Room* (1922), and perhaps even more in the little volume of short stories or sketches, *Monday or Tuesday*, which had appeared in the previous year, we find her experimenting: experimenting with the stream of consciousness technique, experimenting, above all, with the disruption of time.

Time is a problem for most modern writers. They feel bound, cramped, by the necessity of keeping to the strict sequence of events, A followed by B and C following B; they envy the plastic artist his freedom of movement in space, his power of presenting a totality to the eye. Poetry, of course, is freer than prose—poets have always enjoyed a certain license to jump about from present to past and from past to future, to organize their intuitions within a not strictly temporal pattern. But hitherto the novel had been bound. Restricted as it was to the sphere of action, to the telling of a story, it had to present the sequence of cause and effect. The reader wanted to know 'what is going to happen now'; in particular, the Victorian convention (followed by Dickens, Thackeray, and Trollope) of serial publication prescribed a rigid scheme of 'continued in our next' and made development and experiment impossible.

Perhaps the first note of revolt, in England at least, was sounded by E. M. Forster. Tentatively in his novels, and more boldly in the course of lectures which were published as *Aspects of the Novel* in 1927, he criticized the time-obsession in fiction. Indeed, he assailed the story, the plot, itself, as Virginia Woolf remarks in the review she wrote on his book. 'Many are the judgements that we would willingly argue, many are the points over which we would willingly linger, as Mr. Forster passes lightly on his way. That Scott is a story-teller and nothing more; that a story is the lowest of literary organisms; that the novelist's unnatural pre-occupation with love is largely a reflection of his own state of mind while he composes—every page has a hint or a suggestion which makes us stop to think or wish to contradict.' As a reviewer, she had neither time nor space to debate these points; as a novelist, we find them influencing her increasingly. The argument about Scott comes at a crucial point in *To the Lighthouse*. She noted and she pondered. Even within the limits of her review she arrives at

certain highly significant conclusions. 'In England at any
rate the novel is not a work of art. There are none to be
stood beside *War and Peace, The Brothers Karamazov,* or
A la Recherche du Temps Perdu.' She calls upon the critic to
be less domestic and the novelist, the English novelist, to
be bolder.

> He might cut adrift from the eternal tea-table and the plausible
> and preposterous formulas which are supposed to represent the
> whole of our human adventure. But then the story might wobble;
> the plot might crumble; ruin might seize upon the characters. The
> novel, in short, might become a work of art.

There can be no doubt that Virginia Woolf was stimu-
lated and encouraged by *Aspects of the Novel,* with its first
open statement of revolt; but that she had already begun to
put into practice most of Forster's hints some six years
earlier. *Monday or Tuesday,* however, was a mere collection
of sketches. It was in 1925, with *Mrs. Dalloway,* that she
first shattered the time-pattern within the space of a full-
length novel. Here she made the bold experiment of
restricting her scheme to the limits of a single day, a single
district of London, a single in-the-round character (a return
to the Three Unities already signalized in *Ulysses*) while
employing the devices of memory and dramatic counter-
point (Septimus Warren Smith's day is linked harmonically
with Clarissa's, though the two characters never meet) to
avoid poverty and monotony. Later, in *To the Lighthouse*
(1927) we see her playing other tricks with time; in the first
section the action is restricted to one evening, the hours
between six o'clock and dinner, and in fact even these few
hours are fore-shortened to a single moment, for in obedience
to Mrs. Ramsay's 'Time stand still here!' there is a suspen-
sion similar to that imposed by Mr. Weston, in T. F. Powys's
novel, *Mr. Weston's Good Wine,* on the bewildered inhabitants of Folly Down. In the second section 'Time Passes'
the human element is withdrawn; the house is left alone
to decay. In the third section, memory comes into its own
and the present is displaced by the past.

Why, we may ask, this preoccupation with time? Why this ceaseless experimenting with the devices of memory and foreshortening? It is probably not enough to reply that Mrs. Woolf found the time-sequence inadequate to her intuition of reality, though that is an important point for a writer who, as she does, essays to give a this-worldly rendering of an other-worldly pattern or series of patterns or glimpses of patterns. But there is another reason. I think she found the time-sequence inadequate too to the simple rendering of character, to the display of her creatures' inner lives. This is most strikingly demonstrated in her next work, the fantasy *Orlando* (1928), in which the life of her heroine, which in *Mrs. Dalloway* and *To the Lighthouse* had been foreshortened to one day, is stretched out to the perspective of four centuries; in which, too, there is a change of sex from masculine to feminine. All this metamorphosis, this complication and explication, is necessary to elucidate that most mysterious entity, the human spirit. 'One wanted fifty pairs of eyes to see with', Lily Briscoe had reflected in *To the Lighthouse*. 'Fifty pairs of eyes were not enough to get round that one woman with, she thought.' Very well, we can hear Virginia Woolf replying, let us see how many pairs of eyes, in four hundred years, are needed to pluck out the heart of Orlando's mystery. Let us show Orlando as first masculine, and then feminine; first in love, and then loved; first jilting, and then jilted; a man of action and a poet, a woman of fashion and a Victorian lady.

In *The Waves* (1931) the process is carried a step further; indeed, to what we can only imagine to be its conclusion, for further development can hardly be expected along a line which has led, as here, to the suppression of plot, dialogue, and exterior description. *The Waves* presents us with six characters who grow up from children to men and women, but who never, in the novel, address one another, never attain an effective relationship, but move in and out of a pattern as in the intricate steps of the ballet. Counter-pointed against the changing emotions and sensations of six lifetimes is the inexorable process of a solar day. We are presented with a tissue of infinite complexity, in which each personality is mirrored in the minds of the other five and, that multiple image is again multiplied in the great glass of the novel, itself a fractional image reflected from the moving pageant of sea and earth and sky which forms the exordium to each of the nine sections of the book. 'Mirror on mirror mirrored is all the scene'. The undertaking is prodigious, and so, I think, is the effect; but many readers have found the effort of concentration which they are called upon to make beyond their powers. More than any other of her books *The Waves* deserves to be labelled 'difficult'.

Her next novel, *The Years* (1937), is a marking time. There is almost a regression to the early technique of *The Voyage Out* and *Night and Day*. The element of plot returns, there are hints of set descriptions. Time is disrupted, but in no very original manner: we are carried from 1880 to 1891, from 1907 to 1910, and so on, but the result is a series of fragmentary impressions rather than a bold and original perception. It is only with her final (and indeed posthumous) novel, *Between the Acts* (1941), that we get a hint of the new direction along which Virginia Woolf's art is going to develop—a direction which, with its suggestion of a marriage of poetic and prose technique, picks up a note sounded in *Monday or Tuesday* and a thread she had left hanging in her review of *Aspects of the Novel*:

> The assumption that *fiction is more intimately and humbly attached to the service of human beings than the other arts* leads to a further position which Mr. Forster's book again illustrates. It is unnecessary to dwell on her [fiction's] aesthetic functions because they are so feeble that they can safely be ignored. Thus, though it is impossible to imagine a book on painting in which not a word should be said about the medium in which a painter works, a wise and brilliant book, like Mr. Forster's, can be written about fiction without saying more than a sentence or two about the medium in which a novelist works. Almost nothing is said about words.

II

THE LAW OF PROPORTION

I have italicized a phrase in that last passage because it serves to introduce the theme of this second part of my essay. What is the relation between fiction and the service of human beings? What is the *moral* task of the artist?

In the very rapid survey we have just made of Virginia Woolf's work there are clearly several gaps. It is hardly credible, for instance, that between 1931 (*The Waves*) and 1937 (*The Years*), or again between 1937 and 1941 (*Between the Acts*), she should have written and published nothing. In fact, these intervals in novel-writing (and there are others) were occupied in reviewing and essay-writing. Virginia Woolf's critical work, collected in the two series of *The Common Reader* (1925 and 1932) and a number of volumes published after her death, is delightful to read and adds a new dimension to our understanding of her; I regret that considerations of space prevent me from adding in this essay to what I have said about it elsewhere. As a critic, she brought a spontaneous delight and a delicate humanism to the understanding of English literature; her taste was catholic, her discernment rapid and assured. Where she could praise, she did so; but not all she wrote was favourable. She disliked whatever was second-rate, middle-brow, and propagandist. She disliked the commercial novel, she disliked the political poetry of the thirties, she had no patience with cant and pseudo-scholarship. She was a highbrow.

Her occasional writing was not entirely taken up with literary criticism. Part of it was devoted to what we can only call invective. There was this side to Virginia Woolf; and indeed it is a corollary of the sensitiveness displayed in her creative work that she should be vulnerable to pity and indignation. She responded to the horrors of China, of

Spain, of Abyssinia, in a way which we can hardly fathom. To her the remote was not tolerable because it was remote, nor the familiar acceptable by its familiarity. Hence *Three Guineas*, hence *A Room of One's Own*. I do not propose to discuss these books. They should, however, be read, and in reading them I recommend that the reader keep in mind two things: how Virginia Woolf died and this sentence of Schiller's, *Mit der Dummheit kampfen die Gotter selbst vergebens*. With stupidity the gods themselves strive in vain.

It is to her credit as an artist that these sympathies did not blunt her perception, affect her detachment, or upset the balance of her work. They are there, but they are fully absorbed into the stuff of the novel. There are no bits and bobs left over. Now it is here that her writing differs so radically from that of 'the left', the current of action. In speaking of Virginia Woolf's modernity, I suggested aware-ness of the contemporary situation and adequate expression of that awareness as essential 'notes'; I also suggested that there was a third essential: proportion. It is this note that we must now consider. There is a rightness of balance or perspective that enables a novelist to put first things first: to see, in the turmoil of events, the point of rest, the still centre, which gives meaning and brings understanding. We know how the poets mediate this understanding, by symbol and allusion, by music and rhythm; but how is the novelist, weighed down by character and plot, to make it felt? This question links our consideration of the importance of technique and our consideration of the importance of perspective. Let us see if we can answer it.

The modern vogue of the novel stems undoubtedly from the perplexity of our time. The genre has quite lost its odd tang of frivolity. For our grandparents, novels were a species of dissipation, to be classed with romps and too frequent visits to the Zoo. Serenely conscious of the stability of their age, the Victorians devoted their reading hours to Paley's *Evidences of Christianity*, to books of travel, or to poetry. They needed no literary picture of their own time: they could see it (they thought) quite clearly for themselves. But for us the novel is a necessity, like modern hospitals, asylums, or an efficient drainage system. It performs for us, too, something of the function of a home psychologist. We hardly feel that we exist unless we find ourselves within the covers of a book. The cinema, on a cruder plane, has the same *raison d'etre*; and as our thoughts and feelings become cruder, other media will no doubt, in time, entirely take the place of the serious novel.

The first use of modern writing, I would suggest, is to hold a mirror up to the confusions of the age. Better, perhaps, to say a number of mirrors. No single writer is equipped to deal with such chaos. 'Like a ship in a black storm, we fly we know not whither.' On all sides the established things are cast down, on all sides a multitude of creeds call for acceptance. Incessantly, violently, we are buffeted by strange winds of doctrine. It is now, however, that the novelists come to our aid. In the *cameræ obscuræ* of the best writers, the raw material of life (so terrifying in its amorphous actuality) is reduced to manageable proportions. We are given a frame, a scale of reference. Certain aspects of chaos are detached and considered apart from the rest: they are thereby provided with a semblance of order. The writer need not distort, need not impose a false symmetry. The act of selection and separation is enough. In reading the modern novel we pass from one view-point to another— from Lawrence to Forster, from Virginia Woolf to T. F. Powys, from Greene to Golding—as though we walked past a series of windows. All give out upon the same turbulent scene, but each presents us, within the framework of art, with some new aspect of the whole. Lawrence stresses the physical and instinctive, Forster the civilized and the tolerant, Powys shows us the hidden horror of the village, Virginia Woolf the secret places of the heart. Greene presents the conflict of faith and passion, Golding the anatomy of strength in weakness. But through them all (if they do their job properly) there will emerge, whatever their religious or political beliefs, a principle which is *the* principle of art and, in consequence, an important aid to satisfactory living. It is the rule of proportion.

The modern writer (let us say it again) is bound to deal with the events of his time. But in this very immediacy, this contemporaneity, there lies a pressing danger—a danger to that rule of proportion which the good artist must observe. Approaching the raw material of his age too closely, the writer of talent, rather than genius, is sucked into the whirlpool and lost. Lost, that is, as an artist. As a social writer, as a propagandist, he may continue richly to exist. It requires a powerful mind and an intense individuality— in short, genius—to dominate the dangerous stuff of life. Without genius the window (which I have pictured looking down on the foaming waters of the age) splinters as we press against it—and we fall headlong. The artist is submerged, the politician, the theorist takes his place. 'I am really sorry', said William Blake at the beginning of the last century, 'to see my countrymen trouble themselves about politics. If they were wise, the most arbitrary Princes could not hurt them. If they are not wise, the freest government is compell'd to be a Tyranny. Princes appear to me to be fools. Houses of Commons and Houses of Lords appear to me to be fools; they seem to me to be something else beside Human Life.'

They seem to me to be something else beside human life! Exact and pregnant phrase! And what would Blake say, if he were alive today, of the United Nations, of the Hague Court, of planning and nationalization? Precisely the same, I suspect. For these things *are* something other than human life. They are the frame, and only the frame, within which life may be lived. And, alas! they are too often the frame outside which life must be lived if it is to be *lived* at all. Yet it is with the frame that the men of talent are almost exclusively occupied. We remember H. G. Wells, who began his career with an

agreeable flair for writing scientific romances and an obser-
vant eye for the oddities of lower middle class behaviour:
but who afterwards, toppling into this Slough of Despond,
set up as a purveyor of Utopias to the world. We have the
sad example of Aldous Huxley, whose geniune gifts as
satirist and essayist are now obscured under the mantle of a
neo-Brahmin sage. With these, and with many more, the
Moloch of abstraction has had its will. Overwhelmed, they
either perish in the storm or are whirled away by it.

'In the destructive element immerse': Conrad's slogan
is a true one, and essential to the writer. Yes, we must
immerse, but we should not drown or dissolve. We may
write about the eagles and the trumpets, about movements,
about economic realities: but somewhere we must keep a
place for the lovers in their trance of happiness, for the boy
chasing a butterfly, for the old man asleep under the chest-
nut tree. We must observe the law of proportion. Now
this is precisely what Virginia Woolf does. We feel, throughout her novels, the big abstract movements going on: the
feminism of *The Years*, monarchy and the war in *Mrs.
Dalloway*, the pressure of Europe's coming doom in *Between
the Acts*; but these things don't submerge the delicate, exact
understanding and handling of the human situation. Her
people live: they are not Shavian puppets. The individual
is in the centre of the stage. The individual—and the subtle
relations between individuals, what Mrs. Ramsay does *not*
say to her husband, what a gesture conveys to Giles Oliver:

> The wild child, afloat once more on the tide of the old man's
> benignity, looked over her coffee cup at Giles, with whom she felt
> in conspiracy. A thread united them—visible, invisible, like those
> threads, now seen, now not, that unite trembling grass blades in
> autumn before the sun rises. She had met him once only, at a cricket
> match. And then had been spun between them an early morning
> thread before the twigs and leaves of real friendship emerge. She
> looked before she drank. Looking was part of drinking. Why waste
> sensation, she seemed to ask, why waste a single drop that can be
> pressed out of this ripe, this melting, this adorable world? Then she

drank. And the air round her became threaded with sensation. Bartholomew felt it; Giles felt it. Had he been a horse, the thin brown skin would have twitched, as if a fly had settled. Isabella twitched too. Jealousy, anger pierced her skin.[1]

Now it is in order to convey these moments of perception that writers like Proust and Virginia Woolf have forged a new technique of the novel. It is the task of the modern writer to catch these moments amid the increasing hubbub, the diminishing solitude, of modern life. Formerly it was the poets who did it. It was they who explored the secret springs of conduct, who made us see that under the flux of things the great passions still hold sway: love, friendship, hatred, with birth and death, the rhythm of the seasons, the infinite pathos and splendour of man's destiny:

> O what if gardens where the peacock strays
> With delicate feet upon old terraces,
> Or else all Juno from an urn displays
> Before the indifferent garden deities;
> O what if levelled lawns and gravelled ways
> Where slippered Contemplation finds his ease
> And Childhood a delight for every sense,
> But take our greatness with our violence?
>
> What if the glory of escutcheoned doors,
> And buildings that a haughtier age designed,
> The pacing to and fro on polished floors
> Amid great chambers and long galleries, lined
> With famous portraits of our ancestors—
> What if those things the greatest of mankind
> Consider most to magnify, or to bless,
> But take our greatness with our bitterness?[2]

And this is the use of literature in all ages: to show men and women amid the splendour of their environment—and yet, in a moment of passion, of betrayal, of reality, reduced

[1] *Between the Acts.*
[2] W. B. Yeats *Meditations in Time of Civil War.*

to their essential humanity, to the greatness, the violence
and the bitterness of the lonely heart. In what else is Homer,
or Shakespeare, or Dante great, if not in this? Consider some
of the famous lines which colour our waking hours and our
dreams. The magnificence of Dante's Brunetto Latini, who,
though in hell, ran like those who contend for the prize at
Verona:

> e parve di costoro
> quegli che vince e non colui che perde.

And Webster's Duchess, with all her bright world of love
shattered about her: *I am Duchess of Malfi still*. And in the
supreme height, Cleopatra as she presses the asp to her
breast:

> Dost thou not see my baby at my breast
> That sucks the nurse asleep?

It is the poets and the great novelists who reduce us to our
pure humanity, to the forked radish, the unaccommodated
man; and stripped of the trappings of grandeur and vanity
we see ourselves again as we are, solitary, vulnerable, and
transient.

How tremendously helpful this is in a world which tries
to persuade us that the important things are religious beliefs,
social distinctions, political adherences! Let us listen again to
the voice of William Blake. *They seem to me to be something
else besides human life*. On all sides, by the radio, the cinema,
the daily newspaper, we are bludgeoned into disproportion.
From a billion loudspeakers, a million silver screens, the
Antichrist bellows and gesticulates. It is salutary to be set
naked beneath the stars. And it is salutary to see the others,
the big imposing men who seek to dominate us, *sub specie
æternitatis*. Do not let us be worried by them, by their loud
voices, their titles, their decorations. 'Things are what they
are', said Bishop Butler, 'and the consequences of them will
be what they will be: why therefore should we wish to be
deceived?'

Virginia Woolf's standpoint is, above all, this standpoint of reality. It is for this that she praises the Greeks, that she loves Plato.

> For as the argument mounts from step to step, Protagoras yielding, Socrates pushing on, what matters is not so much the end we reach as our manner of reaching it. That all can feel—the indomitable honesty, the courage, the love of truth which draw Socrates and us in his wake to the summit where, if we too may stand for a moment, it is to enjoy the greatest felicity of which we are capable.

But for Virginia Woolf there is not one kind of truth, there are two. There is the truth of the reason, and there is the truth of the imagination. The truth of the reason is pre-eminently the masculine sphere, while the truth of the imagination is the feminine. Together, these make up what she calls reality. Some individuals combine the male and the female modes of perception more impartially than others; these are the artists, the poets and painters who mediate reality to us. They show us how neither the rational nor the intuitive can get on without the other. Mrs. Ramsay and Mr. Ramsay in *To the Lighthouse* need each other. Mrs. Dalloway, in the earlier novel, because she has married a politician, a sentimentalist, is unhappy: with all his kindness, with all the amentities of her life, she is out of touch with reality. Mr. Ramsay is a philosopher; intolerant, egotistical, eccentric, he is yet a better husband than the impeccable Richard Dalloway who is a Member of Parliament. Virginia Woolf agrees with Blake: these things are not human life. Houses of Parliament, Law Courts, the Mansion House: she gives us her picture of them in *Three Guineas*:

> Your world, then, the world of professional, of public life, seen from this angle undoubtedly looks queer. At first sight it is enormously impressive. Within quite a small space are crowded together St. Paul's, the Bank of England, the Mansion House, the massive if funereal battlements of the Law Courts; and on the other side, Westminster Abbey and the Houses of Parliament. There, we

[women] say to ourselves, pausing, in this moment of transition on the bridge, our fathers and brothers have spent their lives. All these hundreds of years they have been mounting those steps, passing in and out of those doors, ascending those pulpits, preaching, money-making, administering justice.

And she goes on to show us how absurd it all is, how unreal. Against it she will set, in *A Room of One's Own*, this picture:

> What is meant by 'reality'? It would seem to be something very erratic, very undependable—now to be found in a dusty road, now in a scrap of newspaper in the street, now in a daffodil in the sun. It lights up a group in a room and stamps some casual saying. It over-whelms one walking home beneath the stars and makes the silent world more real than the world of speech—and then there it is again in an omnibus in the uproar of Piccadilly.

This is not, let us note, the aesthetic attitude; no cult of beauty. Reality inheres in the scrap of dirty paper as much as in the sunlit daffodil. The thing seen is not important in itself, or rather it does not matter what our judgement is of the thing seen. Can we see it without judgement, without choice, with silent awareness? If so, we shall know reality. This is the 'message' of Virginia Woolf's novels; and it is a rather important message. No one was less of a teacher, no one less didactic: yet what she shows us here bears directly on living. To be taught how to see—is not that a great thing? Because, if we can learn to see in this way, there comes (she says it again and again) an extraordinary happiness.

The faculty of seeing directly informs the mind that is concerned for what is, not for what ought to be or will be. That is why Virginia Woolf is anti-religious. Belief of any kind blinds and binds. We cannot see what is when we have theories. It doesn't matter whether the beliefs are religious or political. In an essay called *The Leaning Tower* (originally a paper read to the Workers' Educational Association at Brighton in May 1940, and thus one of the last things she wrote) she discusses those modern writers who inhabit (as she thought) the leaning tower of Marxist class-consciousness.

> If you read current literary journalism you will be able to rattle off a string of names—Day Lewis, Auden, Spender, Isherwood, Louis MacNeice and so on. . . . All those writers are acutely tower conscious; conscious of their middle-class birth; of their expensive educations. Then when we come to the top of the tower how strange the view looks—not altogether upside down, but slanting, sidelong. That too is characteristic of the leaning-tower writers; they do not look any class straight in the face; they look either up, or down, or sidelong. There is no class so settled that they can explore it unconsciously. That perhaps is why they create no characters. Then what do we feel next, raised in imagination on top of the tower? First discomfort; next self-pity for that discomfort; which pity soon turns to anger—to anger against the builder, against society, for making us uncomfortable. Those too seem to be tendencies of the leaning-tower writers. Discomfort; pity for themselves; anger against society. And yet—here is another tendency—how can you altogether abuse a society that is giving you, after all, a very fine view and some sort of security? You cannot abuse that society wholeheartedly while you continue to profit by that society. And so very naturally you abuse society in the person of some retired admiral or spinster or armament manufacturer; and by abusing them hope to escape whipping yourself. The bleat of the scapegoat sounds loud in their work, and the whimper of the schoolboy crying 'Please Sir, it was the other fellow, not me'.

We may regret that Virginia Woolf should bother to castigate these writers of the thirties, but we are concerned here with the implications rather than with the expediency of her remarks. Religion, political beliefs, moral codes: these things are among the blinders and the binders. The writers she mentions are not, in her opinion, interested in what is, but only in their personal responses to what is: never standing still to experience a situation, they react immediately with their stereotyped solution. Thus the reality of the moment escapes them.

In her novels it is the same. We can divide her characters, if we will, into those who are open to reality and those who are shut in—enclosed by various manias of faith, hatred, perversion, politics, morality. The distinction is radical. In the first division we have, to begin with, children. There is George in *Between the Acts*, with whom we opened this essay. There are Mrs. Ramsay's children in *To the Lighthouse*:

> Then the door opened and in they came, fresh as roses, staring, wide awake, as if this coming into the dining-room after breakfast, which they did every day of their lives, was a positive event to them; and so on, with one thing after another, all day long, until she went up to say good-night to them, and found them netted in their cots like birds among cherries and raspberries still making up stories about some little bit of rubbish—something they had heard, something they had picked up in the garden.

The quality of eternal freshness, of wonder, surprise, the coming to each day as though it were the first and only day— this note of spontaneity exists in childhood, and is perceived and enjoyed by those who know. 'One's children so often gave one's own perceptions a little push forward', thought Mrs. Ramsay. In *Mrs. Dalloway* too: the girl Elizabeth, dis- missing the memory of the young men who are already comparing her to poplar trees and hyacinths (the personal, the sentimental, the desirous muddying the clear waters of perception), sees Wren's churches as 'shapes of grey paper breasting the stream of the Strand'. Jacob, in the earlier novel, finds his direct vision blocked, like George's in the later one, by the intruding adult element:

> But there, on the very top, is a hollow full of water, with a sandy bottom; with a blob of jelly stuck to the side, and some mussels. A fish darts across. The fringe of yellow-brown seaweed flutters, and out pushes an opel-shelled crab. . . .
> Jacob was about to jump, holding his bucket in front of him, when he saw, stretched entirely rigid, side by side, their faces very red, an enormous man and woman.

And in *The Years* the pervert under the street-lamp wrecks little Rose Pargiter's fantasy.

But not all adults are closed to vision. There are the

artists—the poets and painters who have kept the innocent
eye of childhood. These see reality whole from the beginning, and express it in its untarnished brightness. Then there
are the young men and women who are not artists but,
because they are free from prejudice and interested in things
as they are, succeed in battling their way towards reality.
We have a whole gallery of these sympathetic figures—
Jacob Flanders, in *Jacob's Room*; Katherine Hilberry, in *Night
and Day*; Bernard in *The Waves*; and many others. All of
them are steeped in the light of Cambridge, the good life
which is devotion to truth and unremitting opposition to
falsehood and cant, the life of scholarship and beauty. But
that light in itself is not enough. It has to be surpassed.
Behind truth there is reality, behind the constructs of the
mind there lies the realm of pure being itself. It does not do
to stay at Cambridge. 'Is there not too much brick and
mortar for a May night?' thinks Jacob, looking round him
at the Great Court of Trinity. In a number of her novels
Virginia Woolf gives us the portraits of people who have,
in one way or another, 'stayed at Cambridge': Ridley
Ambrose and William Pepper in *The Voyage Out*, Mr.
Ramsay and Charles Tansley in *To the Lighthouse*. And
admirable people they are; superior, far superior, to the
successful administrators, the Richard Dalloways and
Colonel Pargiters, who direct the affairs of the great world
from a blank centre while the joy of living crumbles away
from their wives' hearts little by little in an attic room. But
the 'stayers' have become arrested at some point in their
development. They have found truth, they are devoted to
truth, but they have not pushed on to reality. They are
stranded in the realm of the concept.

Now it is here that the third great class of the elect find
their job to do. This is the class of women. The statement,
thus flatly made, seems crass and stupid enough; Virginia
Woolf is far from seeking to canonize her sex as a whole.
What she does, I think, imply, throughout the course of
her writing, is that the feminine personality is closer to

earth, to the simplicity of things, to objects as objects and
not as counters to be talked about; and by virtue of this
concreteness women manage to achieve an adequacy of
response to what is beyond the concrete. The woman's
job, mainly, if she is not herself an artist of one sort or
another, is to free the male intellect from its conceptual
chains, to enrich and fertilize it. Virginia Woolf has been
called a feminist, and of course she was this in one or two
of the less successful of her writings—in, especially, *Three
Guineas*. But more truly we might call her an androgynist,
she puts the emphasis every time on what a man and a
woman have to give to each other, on the mystery of com-
pletion, and not on the assertion of separate superiorities. If
there is in woman a superiority, it is because *she* is the one
to take the first step towards understanding, out of a com-
passion which is almost the Buddhist *karun*; more discern-
ing than the male, she lays her light healing touch on the
source of conflict, the knot of refusal-to-be-what-one-is, and
it loosens. The theme of Virginia Woolf's novels is often
precisely this: the patient effort of the woman towards the
reintegration of the man. His resistance is not always overcome. To show things thus would be to falsify; life, in fact,
offers few happy endings.

We do not, then, find her placing the emphasis, in the
man-woman relationship, on the sexual element; and in this
respect she flows against the main current of modern writing.
Just as she avoids the portrayal of violent action, so too she
largely omits the passional. I don't think she could have
given it us successfully, but in any case it would not have
fitted into the world where she is at home as an artist. For
this is the world of *freedom*. Passion stultifies, distorts, and
corrupts. The people Virginia Woolf shows us as married,
or thinking of marriage, all envisage the problem in terms
of freedom. They are more than ordinarily intelligent
persons. They enjoy a vigorous intellectual life of their own,
and they want to preserve it inviolate. They don't appear to
have very strong physical desires; but they are emotional.

They have a lot of affection to give and to receive. They are fascinated and at the same time repelled by the idea of sharing. They see quite clearly the faults of those they love, but love deeply just the same. A movement of uncertainty, of discovery and relief, runs through the novels as a kind of inner action to make up for the lack of external events.

Virginia Woolf's work presents itself, then, as a study of the inner life of individuals as they exist, first of all, in solitude, and then in society; and as a counterpointing of these aspects. Solitude is a constant theme, the native air breathed by Mrs. Woolf's characters when they are most themselves. In *A Room of One's Own*, she records the importance of seeing 'human beings not always in their relation to each other but in relation to reality; and the sky too, and the trees or whatever it may be in themselves. . . . ' This is solitude. And since even solitude must have a *locus*, since you can't be alone without finding somewhere to be alone, her heroes and heroines enjoy their solitariness, as we should expect, among what Wordsworth called the beautiful and permanent forms of nature. For the point of natural objects is their aloneness. Rocks, plants, rivers, have achieved the secret of forming a society without impinging upon one another's privacy. Virginia Woolf returns again and again to the proud aloofness of natural things. She pictures the tree standing alone in the field through the long summer nights. She sees, in *Orlando*, 'those hyacinths—free from taint, dependence, soilure of humanity or care for one's kind'. Yet, though aloof, they are not inimical to the man or woman who approaches them without arrogance or prejudice. 'Hills and trees accept one; human beings reject one', a character in *The Years* muses.

For a novelist, this taste for solitude plainly presents something of a problem. To be effective within the framework of a story, human beings must care for something more than hyacinths and hills; they must care for each other. How does Virginia Woolf solve this problem? I pass over such explosions of spleen as this from her least genial work,

Three Guineas: 'Is there not something in the conglomera-
tion of people into societies that releases what is most selfish
and violent, least rational and humane in the individuals
themselves?' These words were written under the (to her)
almost unbearable irritation of the Spanish war and the
growing shadow of Fascism. They represent a real attitude
of hers; but not a final or complete one. They do suggest
(what cannot be denied) that her scope is limited, that there
are aspects of human life that she will not touch and situations from which she shrinks back. Her world is a small one,
a world of intellectuals and sensitives, of artists and scholars.
But it is what she does with that limited world that is important. Can she expand it to contain the great paradoxes of life
—love and hate, solitude and society, and the freedom that
springs from loving bondage? If she can, she has done all
that we should require of her.

And here, I think, she does succeed. By reducing the
commitments of her characters to the simplest components
—none of Bennett's bustle or Lawrence's complications for
her—she shows us the pattern of lives which, even while
harmonizing, preserve their individual melodies. A solitude
is kept in the midst of society. Sometimes by a deliberate act
of withdrawal. Virginia Woolf's view is not far removed
from the Blakean doctrine of salvation through art, or the
Taoist technique of *wei wu wei*. 'If one wishes to better the
world one must, paradoxically enough, withdraw and spend
more and more time fashioning one's sentences to perfection
in solitude.' These words from the second *Common Reader*
refer specifically to the writer; but they apply in every walk
of life. Thus Mrs. Ramsay, in *To the Lighthouse*, finds her
arduous duties as wife and mother and hostess bearable only
if she can, from time to time, sink down to be 'a wedge of
darkness'. 'The supreme difficulty of being oneself', as
Virginia Woolf calls it elsewhere, becomes insuperable if
the world is too much with us. But the subtler art of pre-
serving solitude is not by withdrawal, but by fusion. And
this, for Virginia Woolf, is the meaning of love. Human

beings need one another—not for consolation, for protection, to form a closed circle—but for the joy of sharing. The moment of perception is heightened if it can be held in common. 'Some spray in a hedge, or a sunset over a flat winter field, or again the way some old woman sits, arms akimbo, in an omnibus with a basket—these we point at for the other to look at. It is so vast an alleviation to be able to point for another to look at. And then not to talk . . .' But alas! with how few companions can such detached sharing, such shared detachment, be achieved!

There is always the question whether it can be achieved at all. And that is why so many of her novels ponder the theme of compatibility or incompatibility. Can one really live with other people? And still be oneself, free to live, free to develop? The question haunts Mrs. Dalloway and Mrs. Ramsay, Katherine Hilberry and Jacob Flanders, Bernard in *The Waves* and Sara in *The Years*. The answer is given in terms of courage and commonsense. What has been achieved can be achieved. The problem, we note, is radically a woman's problem. It would hardly occur to a man, unless he possessed a large measure of feminine sensibility. And it implies, radically, that absence of passion which we have already noticed in Virginia Woolf's work. We are here in a very cool, still, twilight region. (Many of her most effective scenes take place at evening). The air of detachment, of aloneness, takes on an aspect of poignancy in the more elderly characters of her novels. I am thinking particularly of Mrs. Dalloway and Mrs. Ramsay. In the case of Mrs. Dalloway the poignancy is stressed—the note of regret, of nostalgia for opportunities that are past, the something lost that time in its swift course will not bring back again. Clarissa Dalloway, indeed, has missed her moment, has made the wrong choice in life's intelligence test, has opted for the successful Richard and not for the scapegrace Peter. But even with Mrs. Ramsay, who has achieved so much, whose life is so rich, there is the note of almost unbearable nostalgia—for what?

For what? That is the question. What is missing from Virginia Woolf's picture? For this note of melancholy tells us that something is missing; it is not a healthy sign. The greatest literature is not sad, though it may be tragic. Behind the brilliant, sensitive world she gives us there is an emptiness. And of course we know at once, in part, why this should be. The sensitivity entails the emptiness. Living in the world of *entre deux guerres* and in the world of war itself, she was unremittingly conscious of the fragility of the civilization which is Western Europe, of the transience of the values which her books so shiningly illustrate. But there is more than this. The lack is not only in her world: it is in herself. It is the lack of what we can only call faith. Not the faith that is based on submission to authority, or on wishful thinking—she could never have known that. But faith in the reality of her own intuitions, the faith which is really knowledge in its purest form, for there is nothing more certain or immediate to us than our own 'feel' of reality. This contact she had, intermittently; the mystic (a word which she disliked and for which I would prefer to substitute *noetic*) was strong in her. A dozen passages could be culled from her writing which would worthily stand by the side of Lao Tzü's sayings or the gnomic aphorisms of Blake. But her upbringing was against her. Childhood years in an agnostic household, the company of intellectuals as a woman, had not taken the fine point off her spiritual perceptions, but they had effectively blocked the way to a synthesis.

I will not end on this note of regret. If the sadness is felt it is, like the indignation and the pity, absorbed into the stuff of the novel; and the movement inwards continues even if it is to a centre of which Virginia Woolf could not say assuredly, 'It is there'. The great artist—and she was a great artist—is used for purposes he may ignore or deny. No one can come away from a reading of these novels without feeling that his experience has been enriched, that he has been taught to see more clearly. There is sensationalism in

her novels, the sensationalism of the painter entranced with
colour and form, of the poet drunk with scents and tastes;
but she rises above or rather through sensation to a higher
understanding. She is no Pater. Her delight in the moment,
the vivid crystal of the here and now, is always escaping
into meaning. Just as often, distrustful of metaphysics, she
hauls it back. The reality is always more than the sensation,
but only in the sensation can reality be known. The ripple
of the wave conceals beneath it the world of waters where
swim strange, unthinkable shapes of fish and plant. And—if
I may stretch my sea metaphor a little further—in the
sensationalism of Virginia Woolf there is something one
might call *salt*, a tincture lacking in Pater and his like. The
aesthetes cultivated sensation, she accepted it; the faint smell
of decay is absent. They distrusted the intellect, she worships
it—in its own place. They withdrew to the ivory tower,
she writes *Three Guineas*, preaches feminism. Salt—the
tincture of humour, responsibility, reverence for qualities
not her own—keeps her writing sweet. Though her world is
a limited one, vast perspectives are thrown open. And how
wise she was to limit her scope to those intimate relationships that she knew so well!

It is because of this self-limitation, itself stemming from a
shrewd assessment of her own resources, that her position in
English fiction is, it seems to me, assured. She did supremely
well what no one else has attempted to do. She mapped the
world of the mind—especially the feminine mind—under
certain precise conditions of character and environment. Her
work forms a unity, the unity of a great poem like *The
Waste Land* or *Four Quartets*. Within it we revolve, with Sir
Thomas Browne alone in his study, the globe of ourselves.
'I could never content my contemplation with those general
pieces of wonder, the Flux and Reflux of the Sea, the
increase of *Nile*, the conversion of the Needle to the North;
and have studied to match and parallel those in the more
obvious and neglected pieces of Nature, which without
further trouble I can do in the Cosmography of my self; we

carry with us the wonders we seek without us: There is all *Africa* and her prodigies in us; we are that bold and adventurous piece of nature, which he that studies wisely learns in a *compendium* what others labour at in a divided piece and endless volume.' The Woolfian sphere is neither so bold nor so adventurous, perhaps; but it has its own unity. There, at the mouth of a river in South America, is the little town of Santa Marina; the climate is tropical, but the society might be that of the Cambridge of *Jacob's Room*; a flick of the hand sends the globe spinning to discover a large, ramshackle house in the Hebrides—sea, mountains, barren shore are clearly visible, but as we eavesdrop on Charles Tansley and Mr. Bankes we fancy ourselves back again with Katherine Hilberry in Cheyne Walk. It is good conversation: there is no room for stupidity or violence. The women are wise, witty, maternal; the men, whether old or young, wear rather shabby flannels and tweeds and stump up and down the terrace declaiming Tennyson, debating the nature of things. On the outskirts, it is true, certain sinister figures hover: clergymen, 'irrelevant forked stakes in the flow and majesty of the summer silent world'; power-lovers and soul-destroyers, the Sir William Bradshawes and the Colonel Pargiters, the Miss Kilmans and the Minnie Marshes; or perverts staining a child's memories.

And beyond these figures of darkness there is the circumambient darkness itself, always felt, always pressing in upon the sphere and threatening to destroy it. There is the darkness deep in the nature of things; the tragedy and the waste when Rachel Vinrace dies, her promise unfulfilled (death comes as the end), or when Sally Pargiter is dropped as a baby (death comes as the beginning). These are Acts of God. But there are also the acts of men: the clang of war echoes through the early novels, the darkening horror of Fascism dominates the later ones. The coloured and fragrant sphere vibrates in the chaos. There it hangs, fragile and iridescent. We tremble for its permanence. But there is no need to fear: this bubble is endowed with a surprising toughness. It will stand wind and weather, it will outlive the eagles and the trumpets. And, watching it, we may find that it focuses within its little round essences of human thought and action which escape the net of the blue-print and the interim report. The movement streams inward, towards the still centre. But there is a plane of understanding on which the inward is also the outward, and the particular the most valid representation of the universal. Virginia Woolf's world will survive as the crystal survives under the crushing rock-masses. The Juggernaut which destroyed its creator has no power over this globe of hers and its inhabitants:

> Forms more real than living man,
> Nurslings of immortality.

III. POSTSCRIPT: 1962

In the decade since this essay was first published many changes have come over the literary scene. We have seen the rise of the Angry Young Men in Britain, of the Beatniks in the United States, of the *chosistes* in France, to name only the most prominent among the 'new bearings'. The 'novel of violence' has won hands down over the 'Be Still and Know' tradition. Virginia Woolf has had no successor. That fact in itself does not constitute an indictment; there are some writers so great (the greatest, indeed, need not be named) that there is no room in their circle for others. Swift was an isolated phenomenon, Sterne had to wait two hundred years for his influence to be felt, and its possibilities are still unexhausted. We are just beginning to wake up to Blake. Byron is due for re-assessment.

It must be admitted that Virginia Woolf's stock has fallen in the post-war years. Simultaneous revolutions may clash; as the Renaissance did with the Reformation, to produce the oddest results in the work of Spenser and Milton. Virginia Woolf was 'committed' enough, as *Three Guineas* and *A Room of One's Own* go to show, but her true current, as we have seen, was interior, towards the still centre. A Second

World War, with its aftermath, deflected this current and the interest in subtleties of technique which went with it. We are seeing its re-emergence, perhaps, in a new and fascinating guise, in the present interest in Zen. But so far Zen, unless in the work of Mr. David Stacton, has had no significant literary repercussions. The technical revolution represented so brilliantly by Mrs. Woolf has been short-circuited by insistent political and 'existential' pressures: angry young men and beatniks write in a strangely outmoded idiom. The voice is Jacob's voice.

This is not to say that Virginia Woolf has been without influence. But her infiltration is pervasive, subtle, and unacknowledged. We can see it most clearly in Robbe-Grillet and his school. Mrs. Woolf's intelligence was always more French than English in its lucidity, its poise, its irony. And just as we gave Locke to France and got him back again via Rousseau and the *encyclopédistes*, so Mrs. Woolf is returning to us quite quietly by way of the *chosistes*. Their admirable insistence on the thing seen, on the object *there* in space uncontaminated by impertinent comment, has long been anticipated in a score of passages in the novels, some of which are quoted in preceding pages: and most clearly, perhaps in the short story *Solid Objects*:

> The only thing that moved upon the vast semicircle of the beach was one small black spot. As it came nearer to the ribs and spine of the stranded pilchard boat, it became apparent from a certain tenuity in its blackness that this spot possessed four legs; and moment by moment it became more unmistakable that it was composed of the persons of two young men. Even thus in outline against the sand there was an unmistakable vitality in them; an indescribable vigour in the approach and withdrawal of the bodies, slight though it was, which proclaimed some violent argument issuing from the tiny mouths of the little round heads. This was corroborated on closer view by the repeated lunging of a walking-stick on the right-hand side. 'You meant to tell me . . . You actually believe . . .' thus the walking-stick on the right-hand side next the waves seemed to be asserting as it cut long straight stripes upon the sand.

This is the opening paragraph of a story in which the obsession of an adult mind with solid objects is as convincingly shown as that 'inner darkness' of a child's mind which 'became a hall, leaf smelling, earth smelling of Yellow light' in the first passage of the present essay.

To go a little further afield: to Mr. Patrick White, the Australian novelist who seems to me by far the greatest talent to arise since the death of Virginia Woolf. *Voss* opens with a domestic interior which brings *Night and Day* directly to mind; there is no imitation, the settings are quite different, as far apart indeed as Cheyne Walk and Sydney, New South Wales, but the accents chime, the technique whereby place becomes an interpreter of grace (or its opposite): and might this be an aside on Katherine Hilbery?:

> Already as a little girl she had been softly sceptical, perhaps out of boredom; she was suffocated by the fuzz of faith. She did believe, however, most palpably, in wood, with the reflections in it, and in clear daylight, and in water. She would work fanatically at some mathematical problem, even now, just for the excitement of it, to solve and know. She had read a great deal out of such books as had come her way in that remote colony, until her mind seemed to be complete.

The self-existent life of buildings—particularly of houses—which bulks so large in Virginia Woolf, and their reactions to intruding human presences, also crystallises out:

> Not even the presence of the shabby stranger, with his noticeable cheekbones and over-large finger-joints, could destroy the impression of tranquillity, though of course, the young woman realised, it is always like this in houses on Sunday mornings while others are at church. It is therefore but a transitory comfort. Voices, if only in whispers, must break in. Already she herself was threatening to disintegrate into the voices of the past.

And here, finally, is the return to the assurance of the life of things; with a last twist in the paragraph which brings us

back to the most characteristic of Virginia Woolf's novels,
to *The Voyage Out* and *To The Lighthouse*:

> All this time Voss was standing his ground. He was, indeed,
> swaying a little, but the frayed ends of his trouser legs were
> momentarily lost in the carpet. How much less destructive of the
> personality are thirst, fever, physical exhaustion, he thought, much
> less destructive than people. He remembered how, in a mountain
> gorge, a sandstone boulder had crashed, aiming at him, grazing his
> hand, then bounding away, to the multilation of trees and death
> of a young wallaby. Deadly rocks through some perversity in-
> spired him with fresh life. He went on with the breath of life in
> his lungs. But words, even of benevolence and patronage, even
> when they fell wide, would leave him half-dead.

We may close, then, on a new note: on the possibility of
a fusion of excellences between the novel of reflection and
the novel of action, of the feminine fertilised by the masculine, of a new Conrad arising on a new continent, 'nurslings
of immortality' made flesh and bone in a new, all-inclusive
vision. But the ironic, compassionate portrait which stands
as frontispiece to this study remains for me, at any rate, 'the
marble index' of a kind of greatness which, as Nicholas
Ferrar remarked of the synthesis he established at Little
Gidding, 'might prove a pattern in an age that needs
patterns'.

TITLE INDEX
OF COLLECTED ESSAYS
AND SHORT STORIES
BY VIRGINIA WOOLF

N.B. All titles listed below are essays except those collected in *A Haunted House,* which are short stories.

---

*Katherine Mansfield is the subject of this essay.

VIRGINIA WOOLF

Select Bibliography

BIBLIOGRAPHIES

BEEBE, MAURICE. "Criticism of Virginia Woolf: A Check-List," *Modern Fiction Studies,* Vol. II (1956).

KIRKPATRICK, B. J. *A Bibliography of Virginia Woolf.* London: Rupert Hart-Davis, 1957.

WORKS

Listed in the order of first publication. Place, publisher, and date of the first American edition follow the entry on the first British edition. Current paperbacks and college editions, if any, are also mentioned here. Harcourt, Brace & World, Inc. have most of the major works in print.

The Voyage Out. London: Duckworth, 1915; New York: Doran, 1920. *Novel.*

The Mark on the Wall. Richmond, Surrey: Hogarth, 1917. *Short Story.*

Kew Gardens. Richmond, Surrey: Hogarth, 1919. *Short Story.*

The two foregoing pamphlets were handprinted and published by the author and her husband, Leonard Woolf, at the original Hogarth Press. Reprinted in *A Haunted House.*

Night and Day. London: Duckworth, 1919; New York: Doran, 1920. *Novel.*

Monday or Tuesday. Richmond, Surrey: Hogarth, 1921; New York: Harcourt, Brace, 1921. *Short Stories.*
Reprinted in *A Haunted House.*

Jacob's Room. Richmond, Surrey: Hogarth, 1922; New York: Harcourt, Brace, 1923. *Novel.*
Harvest Books.

Mr. Bennett and Mrs. Brown. London: Hogarth, 1924. *Criticism.*
Reprinted in *The Captain's Death-Bed.*

The Common Reader. London: Hogarth, 1925; New York: Harcourt, Brace, 1925. *Criticism*.
Harvest Books.
Some of the essays in this and in *The Second Common Reader* (see below) were reprinted from *The Times Literary Supplement* and other periodicals.

Mrs. Dalloway. London: Hogarth, 1925; New York: Harcourt, Brace, 1925. *Novel*.
The Modern Library (with an introduction by Virginia Woolf); Harbrace Modern Classics.

To the Lighthouse. London: Hogarth, 1927; New York: Harcourt, Brace, 1927. *Novel*.
Harbrace Modern Classics.

Orlando. London: Hogarth, 1928; New York: Crosbie Gaige, 1928. *Fantasy*.
Signet Books.

A Room of One's Own. London: Hogarth, 1929; New York: The Fountain Press, 1929. *Sociological Essay*.

Street Haunting. San Francisco: The Westgate Press, 1930. *Essay*.
Reprinted in *The Death of the Moth*.

On Being Ill. London: Hogarth, 1930. *Essay*.
Reprinted in *The Moment and Other Essays*.

Beau Brummell. New York: Rimington and Hooper, 1930. *Essay*.
Reprinted in *The Second Common Reader*.

The Waves. London: Hogarth, 1931; New York: Harcourt, Brace, 1931 *Novel*.
Harvest Books (with *Jacob's Room*)

Letter To a Young Poet. London: Hogarth, 1932. *Criticism*.
Reprinted in *The Death of the Moth*.

The Second Common Reader. London: Hogarth, 1932: New York: Harcourt, Brace, 1932. *Criticism*.
Harvest Books.

Flush. London: Hogarth, 1932; New York: Harcourt, Brace, 1932. *Biography*.

Walter Sickert: A Conversation. London: Hogarth, 1934. *Essay*.
Reprinted in *The Captain's Death-Bed*.

The Roger Fry Memorial Exhibition: An Address. Bristol: Bristol Museum and Art Gallery, 1935.

Reprinted in *The Moment and Other Essays*.

The Years. London: Hogarth, 1937; New York: Harcourt, Brace, 1937. *Novel*.

Three Guineas. London: Hogarth, 1938; New York: Harcourt, Brace, 1938. *Sociological Essay*.

Reviewing. London: Hogarth, 1939. *Criticism*.
Reprinted in *The Captain's Death-Bed*.

Roger Fry. London: Hogarth, 1940; New York: Harcourt, Brace, 1940. *Biography*.

Between the Acts. London: Hogarth, 1941; New York: Harcourt, Brace, 1941. *Novel*.
Published posthumously and unrevised, as were the seven following collections, which contain prefatory material by Leonard Woolf.

The Death of the Moth. London: Hogarth, 1942; New York: Harcourt, Brace, 1942. *Essays*.

The Haunted House. London: Hogarth, 1943; New York: Harcourt, Brace, 1944. *Short Stories*.

The Moment and Other Essays. London: Hogarth, 1947; New York: Harcourt, Brace, 1948. *Essays*.

The Captain's Death-Bed. London: Hogarth, 1950; New York: Harcourt, Brace, 1950. *Criticism*.

A Writer's Diary. London: Hogarth, 1953; New York: Harcourt, Brace, 1954. *Autobiography*.

Virginia Woolf and Lytton Strachey: Letters. Edited by Leonard Woolf and James Strachey. London: Hogarth and Chatto and Windus, 1956; New York: Harcourt, Brace, 1956.

Granite and Rainbow. London: Hogarth, 1958; New York: Harcourt, Brace, 1958. *Essays*.

BOOKS WITH AN INTRODUCTION
BY VIRGINIA WOOLF

Victorian Photographs. By Julia M. Cameron. London: Hogarth, 1926.

A Sentimental Journey. By Laurence Sterne. The World's Classics. London and New York: Oxford University Press, 1928.

Selections From the Works of George Gissing. London: Cape, 1929.

Catalogue of Recent Paintings by Vanessa Bell. London: London Artist's Association, 1930.

Life As We Have Known It. By Co-operative Working Women, edited by Margaret L. Davies. London: Hogarth, 1931.

By the Ionian Sea. By George Gissing. London: Cape, 1933.

TRANSLATIONS (WITH S. S. KOTELIANSKY)

Stavrogin's Confession. By F. M. Dostoevsky. Richmond: Hogarth, 1922; New York: Lear Publishers, 1947.

Talks with Tolstoi. Richmond, Surrey: Hogarth, 1923.

Tolstoi's Love-Letters. Richmond, Surrey: Hogarth, 1923.

BIOGRAPHICAL AND CRITICAL STUDIES

DELATTRE, FLORIS. *Le Roman Psychologique de Virginia Woolf.* Paris: Vrin, 1932.

HOLTBY, W. *Virginia Woolf.* London: Wishart, 1932.

GRUBER, RUTH. *Virginia Woolf.* Leipzig: Tauchnitz, 1935.

DAICHES, DAVID. *Virginia Woolf.* Norfolk, Conn.: New Directions, 1942; rev. ed., 1963.

FORSTER, E. M. *Virginia Woolf.* New York: Harcourt, Brace, 1942.

JEHIN, A., AND CELIA SEGURA. *Two Studies in the Contemporary Novel.* English Pamphlet Series No. 4. Buenos Aires: Argentine Association of English Culture, 1943.

BENNET, JOAN. *Virginia Woolf: Her Art as a Novelist.* New York: Harcourt, Brace, 1945.

CHAMBERS, R. L. *The Novels of Virginia Woolf.* New York: Hilary House, 1947.

BLACKSTONE, BERNARD. *Virginia Woolf: A Commentary.* New York: Harcourt, Brace, 1949.

LEHMANN, JOHN. *The Open Night.* New York: Harcourt, Brace, 1952. Contains an appreciation.

PIPPETT, AILEEN. *The Moth and the Star: A Biography of Virginia Woolf.* Boston: Little, Brown, 1953.

HAFLEY, JAMES. *The Glass Roof: Virginia Woolf As a Novelist.* Berkeley: University of California Press, 1954.

BREWSTER, DOROTHY. *Virginia Woolf's London.* New York: New York University Press, 1960.

SIMON, IRENE. "Some Aspects of Virginia Woolf's Imagery," *English Studies,* Vol. XLI (1960).

NATHAN, MONIQUE. *Virginia Woolf.* Trans. H. Briffault. Evergreen Profile Book No. 34. New York: Grove Press, 1961.

GUIGUET, JEAN. *Virginia Woolf et son Oeuvre: L'Art et la Quête de Réel.* Paris: Didier, 1962.

BREWSTER, DOROTHY. *Virginia Woolf.* New York: New York University Press, 1962.

MOODY, A. D. *Virginia Woolf.* Edinburgh: Oliver and Boyd, 1963.

FREEDMAN, RALPH. *The Lyrical Novel: Studies in Hermann Hesse, André Gide, and Virginia Woolf.* Princeton: Princeton University Press, 1963.

E. M. FORSTER

by Rex-Warner

NOTE

THIS essay was published originally in 1950 and reprinted, in a slightly revised form, in 1954. A further printing having become necessary, it was felt appropriate to bring the whole essay up to date. Mr. Warner was unable to spare the time to undertake the considerable revision which appeared to be desirable and I was therefore asked to do it. The result has turned out to be somewhat different from what was intended. Most of the critical material dealing with the five novels has been left as Mr. Warner wrote it except that I have expanded it somewhat and indicated the changes in critical attitude towards Mr. Forster's work that have occurred in the past ten years. Much of the rest has been rewritten, and I can only hope that it does not conflict with what Rex Warner himself would have wished to say.

JOHN MORRIS.

May, 1960.

Study by Jane Bown, Camera Press

E. M. FORSTER

E. M. Forster, only son of E. M. Llewellyn and Alice Clara Forster, was born in 1879.

E. M. FORSTER

Edward Morgan Forster was born in 1879. He was edu-
cated at Tonbridge School, which he hated, and at King's
College, Cambridge, for which he has had a lifelong
affection, and of which he has been for some years a resident
Honorary Fellow. In 1953 he was made a Companion of
Honour.

The two volumes of short stories and four of his five
novels were all written before the first world war. The last
and best known, *A Passage to India*, appeared in 1924, when
Forster was only forty-five years of age, since when he has
published no fiction. Thus, while it is obvious that he has
never been a prolific novelist, it is not true, as is often
suggested, that he has written almost nothing during the
intervening thirty-five years. Since the five novels there
have been two biographies (*Goldsworthy Lowes Dickinson*,
1934, and *Marianne Thornton*, 1956); the Clark Lectures at
Cambridge (*Aspects of the Novel*, 1927); the libretto of an
opera by Benjamin Britten (*Billy Budd*, 1951); some reminiscences of India (*The Hill of Devi*, 1953); and two large
collections of essays, reviews and broadcasts (*Abinger
Harvest*, 1936, and *Two Cheers for Democracy*, 1951). This list
is not exhaustive but it is enough to indicate both the
diversity of Mr. Forster's interests and his continuing
output. Moreover, although in the course of an already long
life Forster has written but five novels, it is important to
note that his later work is almost entirely concerned in one
way and another with developing the themes which play the
major part in his fiction. These, which will be considered
later in more detail, are the necessity for tolerance and the
importance of human relations.

It is sometimes said that E. M. Forster is, in literature, the
last survivor of a cultured liberal tradition which has now

been swept away by two world wars, by economics and by the internecine struggle of dogmatically opposed ideas. If this tradition is imagined as being gentle, tolerant, and intelligent; as containing an intense enthusiasm for the arts and a passionate hatred of imperialism, it is true that Mr. Forster is in the tradition. But he is also capable of standing outside it. He is creative beyond the boundaries of a mild tolerance, more deeply moved and more deeply moving than one who carries for a short period an inherited torch. Though he has influenced many others, he shows in his own work no obvious derivations. His books are filled with a passion for truth in personal emotions and relationships, a hatred for what is false and smug. He accepts the size and grandeur of the world, then with a vigorous modesty comes to grips with it. So a world of art is created and, in its turn, shapes and alters what exists.

Before dealing with the novels it will be appropriate to consider the two volumes of short stories, all of which were written before 1914. One of them, *The Story of a Panic*, is, the author has told us, his first attempt at fiction. In this fantasy Pan visits and puts to flight in traditional fashion a group of tiresome, conventional English people who are on holiday in Italy. All of them are filled with terror; all except a boy who has somehow managed to escape the clutches of convention and good form. He alone welcomes Pan and is thus saved from the fate which befalls his elders. We see here the earliest example of one of the themes which are found in much of Forster's later work. It is developed particularly in the second of his novels, *The Longest Journey*, which, although indirectly and in a complicated way, also depends from an encounter with the genius loci.

Nearly all E. M. Forster's short stories are frankly didactic and much influenced by Greek mythology and ideas. He believes, as did the Ancient Greeks, that the natural passions and emotions of the body are good, and that the world would be a better place if man would enjoy them honestly and without shame. This is a recurring theme in most of

Forster's work, but in the short stories it is more explicitly stated. One of them, *The Machine Stops*, is, however, very different from the rest. It is a reaction to one of the earlier fantastic notions of H. G. Wells, and a remarkable story to have been written so early in this century.

Mr. Forster's short stories have been insufficiently praised, and the student of his work is strongly advised not to neglect them and indeed to read at least a few before beginning the novels. Apart from their intrinsic merit they are exceedingly interesting in that the main themes of the novels, although in a more dreamlike and remote form, begin to appear; are indeed already the basis of the author's view of life.

It is in some ways odd that E. M. Forster should have chosen the novel form in which to expound his views. Of all art forms the novel is the least abstract; it pretends that life is a neat and well-ordered affair. Nevertheless the lives of most of Mr. Forster's characters are not well-ordered; they are a muddle, incidentally a word and a conception of which he seems greatly fond. His novels are much concerned with what a character in one of them has called 'the anodyne of muddledom'. Nevertheless it is the novel in which he has chosen to express his thoughts. Perhaps he himself recognizes the oddity, for in a much-quoted extract from *Aspects of the Novel*, his one work of sustained criticism, he has noted with obvious reluctance and distaste that 'the novel tells a story . . . and I wish that it was not so, that it could be something different—melody, or perception of the truth, not this low atavistic form'.

The short stories are, in some ways, a compromise with this point of view. We might have expected the later work to have progressed in the direction of pure fantasy. The fact is, however, that E. M. Forster is other things besides being an artist. As Peter Burra wrote in 1934, 'he is an artist on the fringe of social reform. He is interested in causes. He has never cut himself off, as most artists sooner or later do, from the political and economic questions of the outer world'. Forster himself has said that 'some closing of the gate is inevitable after thirty if the mind itself is to become a creative power'. And although the 'purpose' is perhaps uppermost in most of his later occasional writings, he has not in any of his novels attempted to preach a sermon. Even *A Passage to India*, although it is 'a book which no student of the Indian question can disregard', is first and last a creative work of art.

Let us now consider the four novels published before the first world war, that is between 1905 and 1910. The world described is naturally different from that of today. The problems and conflicts are, however, the same. Forster's theme is the English middle class in which he himself was brought up. He has written of them that:

> They gained wealth by the Industrial Revolution, political power by the Reform Bill of 1832; they are connected with the rise and organization of the British Empire; they are responsible for the literature of the nineteenth century. Solidity, caution, integrity, efficiency.   Lack of imagination, hypocrisy.

It is the last two qualities which are chiefly satirized in the novels. They are responsible for what Mr. Forster has called the 'undeveloped heart', one of the central themes of his thought. Writing of those Englishmen who are mostly educated at our public schools he has noted that they go out into the world 'with well-developed bodies, fairly developed minds and undeveloped hearts. And it is this undeveloped heart that is largely responsible for the difficulties of the Englishman abroad. An undeveloped heart—not a cold one'.

It is characteristic that this passage should be written with reference to the public schools. Forster himself was a day-boy (he insists upon this distinction in the reference books) at Tonbridge, which was apparently the model from which the 'Sawston' of his first two novels was drawn. He has always detested the public school system and has little if any good to say of it, although it is not known what he would have in its place. It is this system which, more than anything else, comes near to ruining the hero of *The Longest Journey*.

In Cambridge, on the other hand (he studied classics and history), Forster seems to have found the exact antithesis to the public schools. In Cambridge, or perhaps it would be more correct to say at King's College, individuals were respected, not herded together; ideas were discussed, not forced down the throat. 'The young men,' as he wrote in his biography of Lowes Dickinson (also a Kingsman), 'seek truth rather than victory, they are willing to abjure an opinion when it is proved untenable, they do not try to score off one another, they do not feel diffidence too high a price to pay for integrity'.

Yet Cambridge, with its freedom of thought and discussion, its grace and beauty in personal relationships, did not constitute an entire world. Outside Cambridge was not only Sawston/Tonbridge, the world of petty prejudices, of persecution, of vulgarity, but many other worlds as well. There was, for instance, Greece, and it would be interesting to trace the changes and developments of Forster's view of this real and ideal world. There is the half-mystical world of dryads and powers of nature, there is the world of balance and beauty which we enter in several of the short stories; there is the enjoyment of the by-ways of history and, direct result of his civilian service in Egypt during the 1914–18 war, the two books connected with Alexandria, where he first met the poet C. P. Cavafy, whose work is now seen to be part of the tradition that began with Greek tradition. Certainly, both as the result of education and later of experience, Greece has meant much to Forster. In his early work (the short stories have already been mentioned) it is an ideal to be approached with awe and reverence. Possibly too much awe and reverence; for in the novels it is contemporary Italy rather than ancient or even modern Greece that provides Forster with the world to be opposed to his conventional English scene.

The first novel *Where Angels Fear to Tread* appeared in

1905 when Forster was twenty-six. Most good writers are continually, with various modifications, repeating themselves in their different works. Forster is no exception to this rule. In his first novel we encounter most of the themes, much of the method, even many of the characters that are to appear in his later work. There are the two contrasting ways of life—in this case represented by Sawston and Italy; there is the wit and comedy which veil fierce passions and end in acts which are almost melodramatic; there is the search for salvation. There is the characteristic balance and integrity of thought. Though Sawston and all it stands for is condemned, Italy is not sentimentally exalted. There is keen and brilliant criticism of the various snobberies, social and intellectual; there is the insistence both on truth and on the difficulty of discovering it. There are also, I think, some faults which recur in the other novels. *Where Angels Fear to Tread* is, according to Mr. Trilling, 'a novel of sexuality'. I should say that this judgement rather over-simplifies the matter, but it is true that sexuality plays a large part in the story. It is therefore a pity that Forster seems curiously ill at ease with this aspect of reality. Brilliant as he is in his treatment of women on all occasions except when they are in love, he seems to deal with their love scenes as if they were unavoidable plagues. Nor is he much more successful with the men, all of whom, when in love, become suddenly incredible. Nor, I think, does Forster mean this to happen. He might well suggest that love between the sexes is a transitory experience of which much is hoped and from which little comes. But it is not quite this that he does suggest. One is tempted to feel that what he thinks is that this is one of the things that he ought to like, but doesn't. And his women are usually made to answer for it. When they are cosy, they are often good. When they are elderly, they are sometimes given a sort of supernatural importance for which it is difficult to see the justification. When they are young they are usually exceptionally foolish, irresolute or wicked. As such they are admirably presented; indeed the foolish virgins are presented with sympathy as well as understanding—always, except when they are in love. There are similar defects in the male lovers and again one cannot believe that these defects are intentional.

One other point about Forster's method should be made clear before we come to consider the novels. It is, in its own way, a symbolic or allegorical method. The characters mean more than they say; the plot suggests more than is actually there. The main element, for example, in the story of *Where Angels Fear to Tread* is the attempted recovery of a baby from a small Italian town. The baby is half English and half Italian. It is killed by a representative of the Sawston culture. Obviously, with such a plot, Forster is hinting at something further than a mere case of stupidity and cruelty. His horizons expand beyond the limits that he sets for them. His writing, in fact, is poetical, not realistic.

In *Where Angels Fear to Tread* the English middle classes are represented by the Herriton family. Mrs. Herriton, the mother, is a formidable character. Her respectability is her disguise. Under its cover she has, with every appearance of kindness, managed to dominate and to frustrate her two children and to make herself feared by her relations. When thwarted, she will become mean and cowardly. She has unconsciously protected herself from reality, and her effect on others is always bad. Her daughter Harriet is one of the least attractive girls in literature. She is narrow-minded, opinionated, exaggerated in her mean convictions, brutal and blind to everything outside the Sawston conventions. Moreover, she is constantly represented with streaming eyes and with a red nose. Philip, Harriet's brother, is treated with sympathy, though he is far from being a hero. He is a feeble character, an intellectual whose aestheticism is sentimental, faintly cynical, in his own mind superior to others, while in fact entirely cut off from the main sources of life. His history is summed up as follows:

At twenty-two he went to Italy with some cousins, and there he absorbed into one aesthetic whole olive-trees, blue sky, frescoes, country inns, saints, peasants, mosaics, statues, beggars. He came back with the air of a prophet who would either remodel Sawston or reject it. In a short time it was over. Nothing had happened either in Sawston or within himself. He had shocked half a dozen people, squabbled with his sister, and bickered with his mother. He concluded that nothing could happen, not knowing that human love and love of truth sometimes conquer where love of beauty fails.

Yet this unpromising character is, in a way, the hero of the book. One of its chief themes is the development of this undeveloped heart by contact with a different kind of Italy where human love is more emphatic than beauty and where there is a difference between statues and beggars. His experience is shared and partly shaped by another character who is, though in a different way, between the two worlds. This is Miss Caroline Abbott, a young and respectable Sawston girl. She again is transformed by Italy, and again this transformation takes place in two stages.

The Italian world is represented chiefly by the character of Gino, the son of a dentist in a small Italian town. He is good-looking, good-natured, normal in his appetites, totally conventional, but conventional in a Latin rather than in an English middle-class manner.

The two worlds are brought into contact by the visit to Italy of Lilia, Mrs. Herriton's daughter-in-law, whose husband has died. Lilia is a silly, though rather pathetic woman. Of her it is said that her 'one qualification for life was rather blowsy high spirits, which turned boisterous or querulous according to circumstances'. She has been thoroughly persecuted by her mother-in-law (all with the best intentions), and she is happy to be having a holiday in Italy, chaperoned by Miss Abbott.

In Italy she falls in love with Gino and marries him. The Herritons only hear of an engagement and Philip is sent to investigate. Naturally he regards the match as unsuitable.

In fact he cannot imagine that dentists can exist in a country which to him is a kind of fairyland, a compost of ancient Rome, the middle ages and the Renaissance. He offers Gino money to give up Lilia and, if he had arrived earlier, Gino might well have considered the offer. As it is, he is already married. The sight of Philip's face arouses in him nothing but uncontrolled laughter and in his fit of laughter he pushes Philip over on to a hotel bed. Philip, with his pride as well as his sensibility wounded, returns to England, hating Italy and a whole situation which is beyond his grasp.

Sure enough the marriage is, after a short time, a failure. Lilia is bored with the provincial society whose conventions are just as strict though different from those of Sawston. Indeed, as the conventions of Monteriano seem made for men rather than for women, she begins to look back longingly on the world of the Herritons who have now severed all connection with her. Gino begins to develop along lines that she had not imagined. Instead of remaining an agreeable plaything, he becomes an ordinary and, within his conventions, reasonably self-assertive man. He is no longer in love with her, if he ever has been. He is unfaithful to her, and his main desire is to be the father of a child like himself.

Lilia gives birth to a boy and dies while doing so. Previously she has written to the Herritons describing the unhappiness of her life.

The question now is, What is to be done with the baby? The Herritons' instinct is to forget about it. They assume that its father is a villain and its mother was a fool. Here however they are thwarted by Miss Abbott, who insists that, if they do nothing about it, she will adopt the baby herself. The Herritons (or at least Mrs. Herriton and Harriet) then concoct good moral reasons why they should rescue the baby from the terrible fate of living with his own father. It never occurs to anyone that Gino might prefer to keep his child himself.

Somehow (the stages of the plot are complicated here), Philip, Harriet, and Miss Abbott all arrive at Monteriano in quest of the baby. Philip and Miss Abbott soon discover that Gino is by no means the monster that they have imagined. They visit an indifferent but very jolly perform- ance at the local opera. Philip is welcomed as a long-lost brother by Gino and his friends. The baby is admired. Both Philip and Miss Abbott have rediscovered Italy—not in an aesthetic but in a human way. Only Harriet, pertinaciously refusing to enjoy or understand anything, remains totally true to the worst principles of the Sawston world.

The scene appears to be set for a comic ending; but the ending is different. Harriet, with no conception that Gino can love his child, and acting from her religious convictions, steals the baby on her way to the station. Then in an accident, the baby is killed. Philip, with his arm broken in the accident, goes to Gino with the news, and Gino, in an explosion of rage, gropes after Philip in a dark room, tortures him by twisting his broken arm and begins methodically to strangle him. At the last moment Miss Abbott arrives. She appears like a goddess and, almost miraculously, both saves Philip's life and makes the two men again into close friends.

A final surprise comes at the end of the book. The whole Italian experience has brought Philip and Miss Abbott close together. Philip, during their return to England, is on the point of proposing to her, when she informs him that all the time she has been, without ever disclosing the fact to anyone, physically in love with Gino. Her love has not been returned, because he regarded her not as a woman, but as a goddess. Now she will return to Sawston, happy if she can at times talk to Philip of him. Gino meanwhile has married again, finding it rather expensive not to do so.

This first novel of Forster's is not his best. It does seem, however, very characteristic of his art, and for this reason it has been described at length. No description can do justice to the intricacies of the plot, the gradual changes in

the characters, the wit and charm and satire of so many
scenes. It is also worth noting at this stage that in all five
novels there is much recourse to the planting of clues and
chains in preparation for later events. This is one of Forster's
greatest subtleties for generally the clues are so casually
introduced that only at a second or later reading do they
become apparent. This is particularly true of *A Passage to
India*, but even in the first novel the method is already
apparent in the passage which describes the accident, caused
by a storm, which results in the death of Gino's child.
This has been carefully prepared for seventy pages earlier in
a conversation about the weather, but it is done with
such skill that it is not at first obvious.

The next novel, published in 1907, is *The Longest Journey*.
Forster has noted (in a preface to the Everyman's Library
edition of *A Passage to India*) that most readers have dis-
missed it as a failure. There would appear to be reason for
supposing that he himself regards it with particular affection, perhaps because of its association with Cambridge and
his own introduction to the civilized life, although it does
not seem to be obviously autobiographical.

Like its predecessor, *The Longest Journey* is much concerned with contrasting worlds and the investigation of
what is real. It begins in Cambridge with a group of
undergraduates discussing metaphysics (Does a cow really
exist when there is no one there to see the cow?). Into the
enthusiasm and friendliness of the Cambridge world there
comes a young woman from Sawston, Agnes, who succeeds in disrupting the life of Rickie, the intellectual who is
the main character in the book. Like some others of Forster's
characters he is not, however, a very good intellectual. He
finds the metaphysical discussion hard to understand. His
hypersensitiveness is exaggerated by the fact that he has
been lame from birth; and he is as revolted by the memory
of his father as he is attached to that of his mother.

The main theme of the book appears to be Rickie's
collapse into unreality (as represented by his wife Agnes

and the public-school world of Sawston) and his emergence again into the light under the guidance of his Cambridge friend Ansell, and his half-brother Stephen. Once again the climax of the novel is symbolical and violent. Stephen in unembarrassed by intellectualism, often drunk and even unmannerly, but generous about money and in touch with the countryside in a way that is beyond the powers of the other characters. It is only after Rickie's marriage that he discovers that Stephen, who has been brought up among shepherds in the Wiltshire downs, is his bastard brother. Regarding this fact as yet another example of his father's depravity, he is persuaded by Agnes and her schoolmaster brother to disown the relationship and offer a bribe for secrecy. The climax comes when Ansell, who, like Rickie, is also a schoolmaster, in an impassioned but highly improbable speech in the school dining-hall reveals that Stephen is the son, not of Rickie's father, but of his mother. Anybody who knows anything at all about English life will realize at once that a school in which such a thing could happen would not long survive the scene. It is simply not true. We know it and the author knows it, but it is one of his particular qualities that when this passage is read in its context it carries complete conviction; it is like the improbable plot of an opera which, because of the greatness of the music, we do not question when we are actually in the theatre. Incidentally, this is not an isolated example. Shocks of one kind and another occur in nearly all the novels. They are part of the author's deliberate plan. In a significant paragraph of *A Passage to India* we read 'that most of life is so dull that there is nothing to be said about it and the books and talk that would describe it as interesting are obliged to exaggerate, in the hope of justifying their own existence'. We begin to see what Mr. Forster means when he complains that 'yes—oh dear yes, the novel tells a story'.

After the climax of *The Longest Journey* Rickie determines to devote himself to his half-brother. His ambition is to save him from drunkenness; to do what he can to civilize him. But again he finds, as he did in the case of his marriage, that his attempt to enter the real world is a failure. He dies in saving his brother's life, agreeing finally with one of the characters who, just before the incident, has said to him: 'I tell you solemnly that the important things in life are little things, and that people are not important at all. Go back to your wife.'

It will be seen that this novel again concerns a failed intellectual. Rickie cannot be called an attractive character, but he is a character viewed with great sympathy and his attempts to discover reality give him a certain dignity. Forster's satire on the public school world of Sawston is brilliant, and his description of the deterioration of Rickie's character in this world is one of the best things the author has written. The book as a whole is certainly not faultless, but it is by no means the failure it was once thought to be. It has a strangely moving quality and is very revealing of its author's mind.

The next novel is less serious and less passionate. *A Room with a View*, published in 1908, was planned as early as 1903, so it is not surprising that it is more like *Where Angels Fear to Tread* than *The Longest Journey*. It is a book full of exquisite comedy. In particular the women characters, or most of them, are treated with the utmost grace and wit. Yet, together with the comedy there are the usual serious themes and methods. Again we are introduced to a struggle between truth and falsehood, between Art and Life, between a misunderstanding of Art and a misunderstanding of Life. Italy, or the memory of Italy, again plays something of the part it played in Forster's first novel. And a symbolic act of violence sets, as it were, the machinery of the book going. One Italian stabs another in a street brawl, some blood falls on Lucy Honeychurch's Alinari photographs, she faints into the arms of George Emerson—and these events somehow symbolize the problems of the novel. To attempt exactly to define the meaning of the symbol would be to

suggest that it is inadequate. Yet Forster's symbols do
deserve study. It is they which make his writing poetical
and which give to his later work its peculiar distinction.
The blood on the photographs, the more conventional
symbols of unexpected blood relationships in *Where Angels
Fear to Tread* and in *The Longest Journey* lead up to the more
imposing symbolism of *Howards End* and The Marabar
Caves.

As for Lucy Honeychurch and George Emerson, their
problem is simply to get married, and at last a happy ending
is provided. Yet once more it is by no means easy to
discover where Forster stands himself. When Lucy has
broken off her engagement with Cecil Vyse—one of
Forster's few intellectuals who are represented as being
predominantly priggish, conceited and unattractive—she
does not realize that in fact she loves George Emerson.
In Forster's words:

> She gave up trying to understand herself, and joined the vast
> armies of the benighted, who follow neither the heart nor the
> brain, and march to their destiny by catchwords. The armies are
> pleasant and pious folk. But they have yielded to the only enemy
> that matters—the enemy within. They have sinned against passion
> and truth, and vain will be their strife after virtue.

'The heart and the brain', 'passion and truth', 'Eros
and Pallas Athene'—these certainly appear to be Forster's
ideals. But it is not so simple as that. In the end Lucy
recognizes her real feelings and will marry George. At this
point Mr. Beebe, a clergyman who so far has been definitely
on the side of life, who has shown himself tolerant and
understanding, who likes Italians and who will bathe naked,
suddenly turns against the marriage.

This sudden *volte-face* has puzzled most critics. Some have
explained it by suggesting that Forster dislikes clergymen so
much that he could not bear to have one 'good' clergyman
in any of his books. One has too high an opinion of the
author's artistic integrity to accept this solution. Of Mr.

Beebe we read: 'His belief in celibacy, so carefully con-
cealed beneath his tolerance and culture, now came to the
surface and expanded like some delicate flower.' His strong
feeling in favour of virginity is 'very subtle and quite
undogmatic'. It is a feeling that does cast something of a
blight over the general rejoicing of the average reader, and
in it, I think, one finds an example (not perhaps a very
successful one, from the point of view of the novel) of
Forster's reluctance to commit himself finally even to such
obviously imposing slogans as Truth or Life. In a sense
he may be blamed for irresolution; in another sense he may
be esteemed for scepticism. Certainly both faith and doubt,
daring and timidity are characteristic of his art, which is
indeed based on the very difficulty of reconciling opposites.

It is again his problem in *Howards End*, published in 1910.
'Only connect' is the motto of the book; but the connexion, such as it is, is only achieved through deaths and
breakdowns in the triumph of a kind of sexless femininity.

Here the two worlds are represented by two families.
On the one side are the two Schlegel sisters (half English,
half German) and on the other the Wilcox family, tough,
efficient, limited, unimaginative. Margaret and Helen
Schlegel live for 'culture', for the inner life, for personal
relationships. Yet they are aware of the existence of an
'outer life', something different from what appears in the
books they read and in their discussions with cultivated and
leisured friends. The Wilcoxes, on the other side, adept
at the 'outer life', are unaware of the existence of any other
life at all.

Such is the general theme. Needless to say, it is developed
with the greatest subtlety. The efforts to 'connect' are
various and are usually unsuccessful. But here the efforts
seem to have a general urgency and seriousness that make
them different from their counterparts in the earlier books.
Many, including Lionel Trilling, regard this book as
Forster's masterpiece. It stands at the end of a period; for
fourteen years were to elapse before the publication of

A Passage to India. Yet in depth and seriousness, in a kind of massive or pervading symbolism, it seems to me nearer to the later book than to the earlier ones. It is, like *A Passage to India*, far more ambitious in scope than these were. To quote again from the excellent book by Lionel Trilling—a book to which I am constantly indebted in writing this essay—*Howards End* is a novel about England's fate. It is a story of the class war. The war is latent but actual—so actual indeed that a sword is literally drawn and a man is really killed. England herself appears in the novel in palpable form, for the story moves by symbols and not only all its characters but also 'an elm, a marriage, a symphony, and a scholar's library stand for things beyond themselves'.

This is true, and the novel's plot is too subtle for it to be possible to trace here the elaborate symbolisms to which Lionel Trilling refers, the successes and failures of legitimacy and illegitimacy. Perhaps more than any of Forster's novels this is one that would defy any kind of summary. Many of the difficult knots are again cut in scenes of melodrama and violence. Here, however, they are more successful than in the earlier novels, possibly because their connexion with the basic symbolism of the book is more accurate. Thus one can overlook the improbability of Helen's brief love affair with Leonard Bast, and the killing of Leonard by Charles Wilcox is really horrifying.

As for the book's conclusion, the final results of the effort 'to connect', one may not feel wholly satisfied; yet it is fair to say that the book's value is in the definition rather than in the solution of a problem. In the end the Wilcoxes are defeated. One is in prison, one turns in a kind of abjectness to his wife, Margaret Schlegel, who in the end has inherited the symbolic house. It may be said to be a hard-won victory for the inner life, yet, again to quote Lionel Trilling, 'It is not entirely a happy picture on which Forster concludes, this rather contrived scene of busyness and contentment in the hayfield; the male is too thoroughly gelded, and of the two women, Helen confesses that she cannot love a man, Margaret that she cannot love a child'.

There are two great symbols in this book which, in different forms, will re-occur after fourteen years in *A Passage to India*. One is that of the wise elderly woman, in this case the first Mrs. Wilcox. Her main points seem to be a kind of aristocratic indifference to the loves and fears of the ordinary world, and the mere facts of her femininity and perhaps her age. After death she becomes even more important, a sort of goddess or medicine woman, a representative of female and illogical wisdom.

Forster has noted elsewhere (Everyman's Library edition of *A Passage to India*) his belief that music is the deepest of the arts and 'deep beneath the arts'. In using the music of Beethoven's Fifth Symphony as a symbol he has expressed his knowledge and fear of a basic emptiness in reality, a sense in panic and of insecurity, something which vastly widens the scope of his discussion of English social classes. The passage in *Howards End* in which he does this is one of the most significant in all his work.

> It will be generally admitted that Beethoven's Fifth Symphony is the most sublime noise that has ever penetrated the ears of man. All sorts and conditions are satisfied by it. Whether you are like Mrs. Munt, and tap surreptitiously when the tunes come—of course, so as not to disturb the others—or like Helen, who can see heroes and shipwrecks in the music's flood; or like Margaret, who can only see the music; or like Tibby, who is profoundly versed in the counterpoint, and holds the full score open on his knee; or like their cousin, Fraulein Mosebach, who remembers all the time that Beethoven is 'echt Deutsch'; or like Fraulein Mosebach's young man, who can remember nothing but Fraulein Mosebach: in any case, the passion of your life becomes more vivid, and you are bound to admit that such a noise is cheap at two shillings.

The passage is too long to quote in full, but its ending has a special significance. It refers to the last movement of the symphony: 'the wonderful movement: first of all the goblins, and then a trio of elephants dancing; and Tibby implored the company generally to look out for the transitional passage on the drum'.

Tibby raises his finger as the drum passage comes near:

> For, as if things were going too far, Beethoven took hold of the goblins and made them do what he wanted. He appeared in person. He gave them a little push, and they began to walk in major key instead of in a minor, and then—he blew with his mouth and they were scattered! Gusts of splendour, gods and demi-gods contending with vast swords, colour and fragrance broadcast on the field of battle, magnificent victory, magnificent death! Oh, it all burst before the girl, and she even stretched out her gloved hands as if it was tangible. Any fate was titanic; any contest desirable; conqueror and conquered would alike be applauded by the angels of the utmost stars.
>
> And the goblins—they had not really been there at all? They were only the phantoms of cowardice and unbelief? One healthy human impulse would dispel them? Men like the Wilcoxes, or President Roosevelt, would say yes. Beethoven knew better. The goblins really had been there. They might return—and they did. It was as if the splendour of life might boil over and waste to steam and froth. In its dissolution one heard the terrible, ominous note, and a goblin, with increased malignity, walked quietly over the universe from end to end. Panic and emptiness! Panic and emptiness! Even the flaming ramparts of the world might fall.
>
> Beethoven chose to make all right in the end. He built the ramparts up. He blew with his mouth for the second time, and again the goblins were scattered. He brought back the gusts of splendour, the heroism, the youth, the magnificence of life and death, and, amid vast roarings of a superhuman joy, he led his Fifth Symphony to its conclusion. But the goblins were there. They could return. He had said so bravely, and that is why one can trust Beethoven when he says other things.

An interval of fourteen years was to elapse before Forster developed these symbols in another novel. In 1912 he went to India for the first time, and there he found the final symbol for his novels—something altogether more vast than Italy, more inscrutable than an English house. After his return he began to work on *A Passage to India*, but it did not go well and for the time being he abandoned it. Ten years

later he returned to India for six months, taking with him
the opening chapters, with the intention of continuing
them. 'But as soon as they were confronted with the country
they purported to describe,' Forster writes (in *The Hill of
Devi*), 'they seemed to wilt and go dead and I could do
nothing with them. I used to look at them of an evening
in my room at Dewas, and felt only distaste and despair.
The gap between India remembered and India experienced
was too wide. When I got back to England the gap nar-
rowed, and I was able to resume. But I still thought the
book bad, and probably should not have completed it
without the encouragement of Leonard Woolf.'

Possibly the delay was fortunate. Before Forster went to
India for the second time the war of 1914–18 took him to
Egypt where, in various non-combatant jobs, he gained still
wider experience of different races and of European
officialdom. But India was not forgotten, as is shown by
a number of essays later reprinted in *Abinger Harvest*.

Two works came from the Egyptian period. One, published locally in 1922, is *Alexandria, a History and a Guide*.
The history is engaging and provocative; the section described as a Guide is one of the best and most efficient guides
to a great city ever written. The other book, *Pharos and
Pharillon*, is a slighter affair, but it does contain one of
Forster's most perceptive essays, that dealing with the
poetry of C. P. Cavafy, which was previously unknown
to the majority of English readers.

A Passage to India was published in 1924. Part of its
success in England and America was undoubtedly due to
the fact that the novel appears on the face of it to be a
realistic study of Anglo-Indian relations. It is true that
the story begins with attempts, some ludicrous and some
serious, of Indians and English to understand each other,
and that it ends with a failure on the part of the chief male
characters, Aziz and Fielding, to achieve the friendship they
both desire. The propagandist element in this book is
undeniable although one can hardly conclude that it was

written with that purpose. Nevertheless, although that aspect of it is no longer of other than historical interest it was largely responsible for the book's immediate success in England and the United States; there was much in it for both Imperialists and anti-Imperialists to argue about. But it can now be clearly seen that the book is very much more than a study of the British Raj, more even than a study of the difficulties attending upon personal relationships; it is in fact Forster's most philosophical novel. Although the story is straightforward, has a background of realism, and contains a brilliant satire of that English public-school behaviour this author so particularly detests, what really moves the mind in this book is the characteristic indecision, the contrast between a kind of hope and the 'panic and emptiness' that seemed in the India of those days to have acquired an almost physical reality. Can any faith exist, once this panic and emptiness is admitted? Forster will not precisely answer the question. It is in the posing of it that he succeeds in writing his last and greatest novel.

With regard to this underlying question the character of Mrs. Moore is of the greatest importance. She comes to India with Adela Quested, who, it is expected, will marry her son Ronny, a British official. She is kind and understanding, able even to make contact with the Indians. Speaking sincerely, she pronounces 'God . . . is . . . love' and recommends 'Good will and more good will and more good will'. And, as the book proceeds, she somehow becomes invested with almost supernatural qualities of wisdom. Her sympathy with an insect, a wasp, binds her in a mystical way with the Hindu, Professor Godbole. Her assumed sympathy with Aziz makes her in the end into a kind of goddess, acclaimed as 'Esmiss Esmoor' by the crowd in the streets during Aziz's trial. Yet, from the point of view of the liberal and of the Christian, her character throughout changes for the worse.

At a tea party Professor Godbole sings a religious song. It is a prayer to the Lord of the Universe:

'He refuses to come. This is repeated several times,' announced the Professor.

'But he comes in some other song, I hope?' said Mrs. Moore gently.

'Oh, no, he refuses to come,' repeated Godbole, perhaps not understanding her question. 'I say to Him, come, come, come, come, come, come. He neglects to come.'

It is a vision quite different from that of liberal Christianity. As the hot weather comes, as the young people quarrel and make it up again, she seems to move into a different, a more impersonal, an emptier world. We are told:

> She felt increasingly (vision or nightmare?) that, though people are important the relations between them are not, and that in particular too much fuss has been made over marriage; centuries of carnal embracement, yet man is no nearer to understanding man.

The same idea occurs later, after her terrifying experience in the Marabar cave. She says to her son, who is convinced that an attempt has been made to rape his fiancée:

> 'Why all this marriage, marriage? . . . The human race would have become a single person centuries ago if marriage was any use. And all this rubbish about love, love in a church, love in a cave, as if there is the least difference.'

These ideas seem so extraordinary as to deserve comment. It is difficult to believe that many lovers, married or not, can have regarded their 'carnal embracements' as being steps in the direction of the organization of the United Nations. Yet it is implied that this should have been the result. In some respects Mrs. Moore here may remind us of a more mystical Mr. Beebe. Distrust of sex amounts here almost to a hatred of it. It is too dangerous or too boring an excursion into 'the outer life'. Characteristic of Forster's own attitude is the parenthetical question, 'vision or nightmare?'

Perhaps more brilliantly written than any other passage in this book is the account of the visit to the Marabar caves and of a landscape that impresses the mind with the over-whelming sensation of panic and emptiness. It is in one of these caves that Mrs. Moore is overcome with panic. 'Some vile naked thing struck her face and settled on her mouth like a pad.' This, we learn, is only a baby which its mother is carrying on her hip. Then there is the echo. As she remembers it afterwards she reflects on the noise 'boum' or 'ou-boum' which 'coming at a moment when she chanced to be fatigued . . . had managed to murmur, "Pathos, piety, courage—they exist, but are identical, and so is filth. Everything exists, nothing has value" '. And then 'suddenly at the edge of her mind, religion reappeared, poor little talkative Christianity, and she knew that all its divine words from "Let there be Light", to "It is finished" only amounted to "boum" '.

And from this moment on Mrs. Moore, by all rational standards, deteriorates rapidly. She becomes cross and irritable; she will do nothing to help the innocent Aziz or the hysterical Adela. Her indifference is not saintly, yet, after her death, she lives, as did Mrs. Wilcox, as a pervading influence on the minds and characters of others.

From the outlook of liberal rationalism it may seem impossible to justify this strange figure—a wise woman without any evident wisdom, a Christian lapsed into emptiness, a kind of Magna Mater the echo of whose drum is not ecstatic, though she seems to exact from her worship-pers a willing or reluctant emasculation. It is a process that we have seen in the cases of Margaret Schlegel and Mr. Wilcox. It is a process we have seen in the relations of Rochester and Jane Eyre.

On the other hand it may be said that Mrs. Moore is a link between Christianity and the atmosphere of barely understood Hinduism with which the book ends. She is a sacred memory both to the Moslem, Aziz, and to Godbole, the Hindu. Her children, one of whom marries Fielding, the only 'good' Englishman, are interested in Hinduism. True that Fielding is not wholly happy with this girl. She is, he says, 'after something', and we are told that 'he knew that his wife did not love him as much as he loved her'. Yet this state of affairs, combined with a common understanding of some aspects of Indian mysticism, seems to meet with the author's approval. 'In the language of theology', he says, 'their union had been blessed'. It does not appear to be any great beatification; and indeed, though much is condemned, nothing is really 'blessed' in this brilliant and perplexing book where vision and nightmare tread close upon each other's heels and often go hand in hand.

Two minor, but nevertheless extremely interesting aspects of *A Passage to India* are worth noting. The first, perhaps apparent only to those who have lived in India, is the exactness of Mr. Forster's observation of the Indian scene and the accuracy with which he has recorded the speech of his Indian characters, who use the English language with a rhythm different from those whose mother-tongue it is. The other point is the prophetic nature of the closing paragraph of the novel which, in 1924, must have seemed to many people, fantastically unrealistic:

India a nation! What an apotheosis! Last comer to the drab nineteenth-century sisterhood! Waddling in at this hour of the world to take her seat! She, whose only peer was the Holy Roman Empire, she shall rank with Guatemala and Belgium perhaps! Fielding mocked again. And Aziz in an awful rage danced this way and that, not knowing what to do, and cried: 'Down with the English, anyhow. That's certain. Clear out, you fellows, double quick, I say. We may hate one another, but we hate you most. If I don't make you go, Ahmed will, Karim will, if it's fifty five-hundred years we shall get rid of you; yes, we shall drive every blasted Englishman into the sea, and then'—he rode against him furiously—'and then,' he concluded, half kissing him, 'you and I shall be friends.'

'Why can't we be friends now?' said the other, holding him affectionately. 'It's what I want. It's what you want.'

But the horses didn't want it—they swerved apart; earth didn't want it, sending up rocks through which riders must pass in single file; the temples, the tank, the jail, the palace, the birds, the carrion, the Guest House, that came into view as they issued from the gap and saw Mau beneath; they didn't want it, they said in their hundred voices: 'No, not yet,' and the sky said: 'No, not there.'

In *A Passage to India* we can observe, in a heightened and perfected form, all the qualities which make the four earlier novels so memorable. It also contains the author's considered view of life, a view that he has not changed fundamentally in the thirty-six years since the book was published. To understand this is perhaps to understand why Forster has written no more novels.

Aspects of the Novel, the printed version of the Clark lectures, delivered under the auspices of Trinity College, Cambridge, was published in 1927. It reveals, as one would expect, a keen and individual mind, and a love of great literature which Forster is successful in communicating to the reader. It is an attitude which is not in favour with many of the younger generation of present-day critics. It may well be that *Aspects of the Novel* is not 'criticism' of the highest order; nevertheless, it is full of charm, interest, and urbanity. In an introductory note Forster points out that the original lectures were 'informal, indeed talkative, in their tone, and it seemed safer when presenting them in book form not to mitigate the talk, in case nothing should be left at all'. That was written in the days before broadcasting had attained to its present universality, but it is an interesting indication of Forster's early interest in the spoken word.

That there is a marked difference between the written and the spoken word is so obvious that it is hardly worth mentioning but for the fact that many otherwise highly intelligent and gifted authors and others seem unable to make the distinction. Not so E. M. Forster who from the beginning turned out to be a natural broadcaster; one who, like his near-contemporary, Sir Max Beerbohm, now became known through this new medium, to a vast new audience, many of whom had not previously read his novels. He has published many of his broadcasts in *Abinger Harvest* and *Two Cheers for Democracy*. These two collections are

marked by common sense, great wit and scholarship, and
if a few, by present-day standards, appear to be over-
whimsical, they have a distinct period charm. On subjects
about which he feels deeply Forster can be quite uncom-
promising: there is, for example, the much-quoted phrase
from the essay in which he has described his beliefs ('I hate
the idea of causes, and if I had to choose between betraying
my country and betraying my friend, I hope I should have
the guts to betray my country.').

Forster's two biographies are separated by more than
twenty years, and both are, in a sense, acts of piety. *Goldsworthy Lowes Dickinson* was published in 1934. Forster knew
Lowes Dickinson, who was seventeen years his senior, for
thirty-five years. The parts of his book which deal with
Dickinson as a philosopher and a publicist are not as
Forster himself realized at the time of writing entirely
satisfactory; they deal with subjects outside his range of
interests. Nevertheless the book gives a remarkably intimate
picture of life at Cambridge in the early years of the century.
It is also a tribute to that particular spirit which has always
been a feature of life at King's College, where, perhaps more
easily than in other places, the young and the old are
encouraged to meet on equal terms. In his day Lowes
Dickinson was a legendary figure at King's, as Forster
himself has now become.

Marianne Thornton, published in 1956, is a book of more
limited interest, being the life of the author's great-aunt,
who was born in 1797 and died in 1887. Its most valuable
chapters are those towards the end which contain some
recollections of Forster's own early childhood, but the
book as a whole gives a delightful picture of a very remarkable woman. When Marianne Thornton died she
left Forster £8,000 which, he tells us, was the salvation
of his life. 'Thanks to it, I was able to go to Cambridge—
impossible otherwise, for I failed to win scholarships.
After Cambridge I was able to travel for a couple of years,
and travelling inclined me to write. . . . I am thankful to

Marianne Thornton; for she and no one else made my career as a writer possible, and her love, in a more tangible sense, followed me beyond the grave.'

The Hill of Devi appeared in 1953. This short book describes the author's extraordinary career at the court of an Indian Maharaja, to whom he most improbably acted as Private Secretary for six months in 1921. It is composed partly of letters written at the time to his mother and friends at home and partly of subsequent reminiscence. Some critics have found *The Hill of Devi* an enigmatic book, but on the surface it is one of Forster's most straightforward works. It is of great value as a source-book for *A Passage to India*.

Important and indeed delightful though Forster's miscellaneous writings are, it seems probable that his ultimate reputation will rest upon the five novels. It will be seen that their message, if they can be said to have a message, is not easy and is not entirely liberal. Good sense and good will may seem to be his standards, and often he appears to be writing in the liberating tradition of those who in the first quarter of this century believed in the imminent overthrow of injustice, intolerance, and conventional stupidity. But his novels go further than this. They penetrate the boundaries of deep dissatisfaction and despair; and, though they bring back nothing that seems either flashily or immediately valuable, no key to understanding, no quick hope of amelioration, nevertheless the mind that has visited his world is wider for the experiences of vision or of nightmare or of both.

E. M. FORSTER

Select Bibliography

BIBLIOGRAPHIES

GERBER, HELMUT E. "E. M. Forster: An Annotated Checklist of Writings About Him," *English Fiction in Transition,* Vol. II (1959).

BEEBE, MAURICE, AND JOSEPH BROGUNIER. "Criticism of E. M. Forster: A Selected Checklist," *Modern Fiction Studies,* Vol. VII (1961).

COLLECTED SHORT STORIES

The Collected Tales. London: Sidgwick and Jackson, 1948; New York: Knopf, 1947.
The British edition is entitled *Collected Short Stories.*

SEPARATE WORKS

Listed in the order of first publication. Place, publisher and date of the first American edition follow the entry on the first British edition. Current paperbacks and college editions are also mentioned here, if any. Most of the major works are in print.

Where Angels Fear to Tread. London: Blackwood, 1905; New York: Knopf, 1905. *Novel.*
Vintage Paperbacks.

The Longest Journey. London: Blackwood, 1907; New York: Knopf, 1907. *Novel.*
Vintage Paperbacks; The World's Classics (with an introduction by the author).

A Room with a View. London: Arnold, 1908; New York: Knopf, 1908. *Novel.*
Vintage Paperbacks.
Dramatized by Stephen Tait and K. Allott (London: Arnold, 1951).

Howards End. London: Arnold, 1910; New York: Knopf, 1910. *Novel.*
Vintage Paperbacks.

The Celestial Omnibus and Other Stories. London: Sidgwick and Jackson,
1911; New York: Knopf, 1911. *Short Stories.*
Contains: "The Story of a Panic," "The Other Side of the Hedge,"
"The Celestial Omnibus," "Other Kingdom," "The Curate's Friend,"
"The Road from Colonus."

The Story of the Siren. Richmond, Surrey: Hogarth, 1920. *Short Story.*
Handprinted and published by Leonard and Virginia Woolf at the
original Hogarth Press. Reprinted in *The Eternal Moment and Other
Stories,* 1928, and in *The Collected Tales,* 1947.

"Notes on Egypt," *The Government of Egypt: Recommendations by a Com-
mittee of the International Labour Research Department.* London: 1920.
History.

Alexandria: A History and a Guide. Alexandria: Whitehead Morris, 1922.
History.
Anchor Paperbacks.

Pharos and Pharillon. Richmond, Surrey: Hogarth, 1923; New York:
Knopf, 1923. *History.*
Published by Leonard and Virginia Woolf at the original Hogarth
Press.

A Passage to India. London: Arnold, 1924; New York: Harcourt, Brace,
1924. *Novel.*
Everyman's Library (with an introduction by Peter Burra and notes
by Forster himself); Harbrace Modern Classics.
Dramatized with the approval of the author by Santha Rama Rau
(London: Arnold, 1960; New York: Harcourt, Brace, 1961).

Anonymity: An Enquiry. London: Hogarth, 1925. *Criticism.*
Reprinted in *Two Cheers for Democracy,* 1951.

Aspects of the Novel. London: Arnold, 1927; New York: Harcourt, Brace,
1927. *Criticism.*
Harvest Books.
The Clark Lectures at Cambridge, 1927.

The Eternal Moment and Other Stories. London: Sidgwick and Jackson,
1928; New York: Harcourt, Brace, 1928. *Short Stories.*
Contains: "The Machine Stops," "The Point of It," "Mr. Andrews,"
"Co-ordination," "The Story of the Siren," "The Eternal Moment."
Reprinted in *The Collected Tales,* 1947.

A Letter to Madan Blanchard. London: Hogarth, 1931; New York: Harcourt, Brace, 1932. *Belles Lettres.*
Reprinted in *Two Cheers for Democracy,* 1951.

Goldsworthy Lowes Dickinson. London: Arnold, 1934; New York: Harcourt, Brace, 1934. *Biography.*

Abinger Harvest: A Miscellany. London: Arnold, 1936; New York: Harcourt, Brace, 1936. *Essays.*
A collection of about eighty essays and articles contributed to English and American periodicals.

What I Believe. London: Hogarth, 1939. *Political.*
Reprinted in *Two Cheers for Democracy,* 1951.

Reading as Usual. London: Tottenham Public Library, 1939. *Criticism.*

Nordic Twilight. London: Macmillan, 1940. *Political.*
A "Macmillan War Pamphlet."

England's Pleasant Land. London: Hogarth, 1940. *Pageant Play.*

Virginia Woolf. Cambridge: University Press, 1942; New York: Harcourt, Brace, 1942. *Criticism.*
The Rede Lecture at Cambridge, 1941. Reprinted in *Two Cheers for Democracy,* 1951.

"Edward Gibbon," *Talking to India: A Selection of English Language Broadcasts to India.* Edited by George Orwell. London: Allen and Unwin, 1943. *Broadcast Talk.*

"Tolstoy's Birthday," *Talking to India: A Selection of English Language Broadcasts to India.* Edited by George Orwell. London: Allen and Unwin, 1943. *Broadcast Talk.*

The Development of English Prose Between 1918 and 1939. Glasgow: Jackson, 1945. *Criticism.*
The W. P. Ker Memorial Lecture delivered at Glasgow University, 1944. Reprinted in *Two Cheers for Democracy,* 1951.

Billy Budd. An Opera in Four Acts, adapted (with Eric Crozier) for Benjamin Britten from the story by Herman Melville. London and New York: Boosey and Hawkes, 1951. *Libretto.*

Two Cheers for Democracy. London: Arnold, 1951; New York: Harcourt, Brace, 1951. *Essays.*
A collection of essays, articles, broadcasts, etc. A number of E. M. Forster's occasional writings and articles remain uncollected.
Harvest Books.

The Hill of Devi. London: Arnold, 1953; New York: Harcourt, Brace, 1953. *Travel.*

Marianne Thornton. London: Arnold, 1956; New York: Harcourt, Brace, 1956. *Biography.*

"Indian Entries from a Diary," *Harper's Magazine* (February, 1962).
Entries from Forster's private diary.

BOOKS WITH AN INTRODUCTION
BY E. M. FORSTER

The Aeneid of Virgil. Trans. E. Fairfax Taylor. London: Dent, 1906.

Original Letters from India, 1799–1815. By Mrs. Eliza Fay. London:
Hogarth, 1931.
With notes by Forster.

Flowers and Elephants. By Constance Sitwell. London: Cape, 1937.

The Life of George Crabbe. The World's Classics. London and New York:
Oxford University Press, 1932.

Twenty Years A-Growing. By Maurice O'Sullivan. London: Chatto and
Windus, 1933.

Untouchable. By Mulk Raj Anand. London: Wishart, 1935.

Letters from John Chinaman and Other Essays. By G. Lowes Dickinson.
London: Allen and Unwin, 1939.

The Banned Books of England. By Alec Craig. London: Allen and Unwin,
1937.

Diamonds to Sit On. By I. A. Il'f and E. P. Petrov. Translated by E. Hill
and D. Mudie. London: Labour Book Service, 1940.

Cambridge Anthology. Edited by Peter Townsend. London: Hogarth,
1952.

Tom Barber. By Forest Reid. New York: Pantheon Books, 1955.

The Warm Country. By Donald Windham. New York: Scribner, 1962.

Two Stories and a Memoir. By Guiseppe di Lampedusa. New York:
Pantheon Books, 1962.

BIOGRAPHICAL AND CRITICAL STUDIES

RICHARDS, I. A. "Passage to Forster," *Forum* (December, 1927).

BELGION, MONTGOMERY. "The Diabolism of E. M. Forster," *The Criterion*, Vol. XIV (October, 1934).

BURRA, PETER. "The Novels of E. M. Forster," *The Nineteenth Century
and After*, Vol. CXVI (November, 1934).
Reprinted as an Introduction to the Everyman's Library edition of
A Passage to India, New York: Dutton, 1942.

LEAVIS, F. R. "E. M. Forster," *Scrutiny*, Vol. VII (September, 1938).

MACAULAY, ROSE. *The Writings of E. M. Forster.* New York: Harcourt, Brace, 1938.

PELLOW, J. D. C. "The Beliefs of Mr. Forster," *Theology* (April, 1940).

BROWN, E. K. "The Revival of E. M. Forster," *Yale Review,* Vol. XXXIII (N.S.) (June, 1944).

TRILLING, LIONEL. *E. M. Forster: A Study.* Norfolk, Conn.: New Directions, 1944.

AULT, P. "Aspects of E. M. Forster," *The Dublin Review,* Vol. CCXIX (1946).

McCONKEY, JAMES. *The Novels of E. M. Forster.* Ithaca: Cornell University Press, 1957.

OLIVER, HAROLD J. *The Art of E. M. Forster.* New York: Cambridge University Press, 1960.

CREWS, FREDERICK C. *E. M. Forster: The Perils of Humanism.* Princeton: Princeton University Press, 1962.

GRANSDEN, KARL W. *E. M. Forster.* Evergreen Pilot Book. New York: Grove, 1962.

BEER, JOHN. *The Achievement of E. M. Forster.* New York: Barnes and Noble, 1963.

SHAHANE, V. A. *E. M. Forster: A Reassessment.* Delhi, India; Kitab Mahal, 1963.

KATHERINE MANSFIELD

by Ian A. Gordon

KATHERINE MANSFIELD

From a portrait painted in 1918 by Anne Estelle Rice. *Reproduced courtesy of the National Art Gallery, Wellington, New Zealand.*

¶ KATHLEEN BEAUCHAMP, who wrote under the pseudonym Katherine Mansfield, was born at Wellington, New Zealand, on 14 October 1888. She died near Fontainebleau on 9 January 1923.

KATHERINE MANSFIELD

I

FOR some centuries now the Englishman has been a considerable traveller. War, adventure, commercial instincts, empire-building, the selfless missionary spirit, a profound faith in the English way of life (and at times a profound distaste for it), sometimes mere curiosity have all sent generations of Englishmen beyond the seas. Most of these wrote nothing except letters to their families; many of them not even that. But from all these centuries of foreign adventures English literature has profited, emerging always with fresh experiences and on occasion with new insight. Two main themes can be detected in this literature of life overseas. The first, and more obvious, is the undisguised and uninhibited delight in expanded horizons that gives freshness and gusto to writers otherwise as different as Smollett and Marryat and Graham Greene. The second appears in more introspective writers, who—placed in a foreign setting—turn their eyes resolutely homewards: Stevenson in Samoa remembering Edinburgh with affection, Joyce in Switzerland fascinated though appalled by his native Dublin, the usually unsentimental Kipling recalling his Devonshire schooldays. The theme of exile with its elegiac undertones is seldom far from the thoughts of the apparently confident Englishman on his journeys.

To this second group belongs Katherine Mansfield, though her affinity to these manifest exiles has seldom been recognized. It is, however, the key to a full understanding of her writing. She was a third-generation New Zealander, who received her childhood education in her own country. After further schooling in London, she went back unwillingly to New Zealand with the single-minded intention of returning with all speed to the literary capital. Wearing down her family's resistance, she was back in London within a couple of years. The remainder of her life was spent there and in the south of England, with longer and longer periods on the Continent as her health deteriorated. She did not return to New Zealand, and for some years felt little but her adolescent contempt for the narrow round of colonial life in its early twentieth-century capital of seventy thousand inhabitants. But events caught up with her. The glittering prizes only came her way when they had ceased to matter. Life, if it never singed her wings, certainly burnt her fingers, not once but several times. A reunion with her brother, shortly afterwards killed in the War, completed her enlightenment, and in her middle twenties, a mature and experienced—almost too experienced—woman, she came to recognize that a New Zealander can be as much of an exile in England as an Englishman on an island in the Pacific. From the moment of that discovery the note of elegy entered her work, and she turned for her themes to her origins. All of her best work dates from this point.

The editions of her writings do not make it easy to follow this development. Her earliest volume, *In a German Pension*, was brought out by an obscure publisher and, attracting little attention, went out of print. After her death in 1923, when her reputation was probably reaching its highest point, this resentful and ill-natured volume was reprinted, in 1926, somewhat to the disturbance of readers who were now familiar only with her finished and sensitive work in New Zealand stories like *The Garden Party*. Meanwhile the publication in 1924 of *Something Childish and Other Stories* (in America, entitled *The Little Girl*), which contained a mixture of stories of various dates from some written shortly before her death at the age of thirty-four to one written when she was nineteen, had further confused any but the most careful reader bent on following the pattern of her development, whether in technique or in theme. The collected edition of her work casts no further light. It merely reprints, still as separate entities, each of her separately published volumes; most of the stories are undated, and the dates on others are demonstrably false. In any subsequent edition, one would hope that the stories will be printed in the order of composition, or at least that this information be made available in a brief but accurate appendix.

It is not that the precise date of composition of any one story matters in itself. But it is important before making a critical judgement on a story to know where it fits into her work. The chronological sequence is important for another reason. Katherine Mansfield to a degree almost unparalleled in English fiction put her own experiences into her stories. She wrote of nothing that did not directly happen to her, even when she appeared to be at her most imaginative and fanciful. Her stories, read in their order of composition, gain force and significance, and are illuminated at all points by the events of her own history. Her whole work read in this manner emerges as a kind of *recherche du temps perdu*, a remembrance of things past in a distant dominion.

II

Katherine Mansfield was born in 1888 in Wellington, New Zealand. Her father, Harold (later Sir Harold) Beauchamp, was a merchant who combined a shy sensitivity at home with a ruthless drive in his business affairs. She grew up in a family group of two older sisters and a younger brother, with a grandmother and unmarried aunts among the adult members. From the village school she went via the Girls' High School to a private school for young ladies, and then (the family ambition and fortunes still rising) to four years at Queen's College, Harley Street, London. Returning to Wellington in 1906, her head filled with Oscar Wilde and the glamour of the literary life, she sulked, and refused to play the part of the accomplished middle-class daughter back from finishing-school. With an allowance from her father (which continued throughout her life) she left for London in 1908 to establish herself as a writer. She was nineteen. She had published a few sketches. All she required was experience. The process was not pleasant. Within a short time she was in retreat, seeking one refuge after another. What she could not know at the time, and came to recognize only after years of despair, was that when she left her own country at the age of nineteen she had already experienced all that she required. The material for her finest work lay in the family group she had abandoned and the colonial town she had so contemptuously left behind.

Within a year of her arrival in London she was pregnant; married, and not to the father of her child; had left her husband, and been packed off by an unsuspecting mother to recuperate in a Bavarian village. The child miscarried; the incident was closed. But all of this lay behind the snarling ill-humour of her stories of this period. They were first printed in periodical form during 1910, after her return, and (if one excepts *A Modern Soul*) form the first seven stories in her 1911 volume, *In a German Pension*. The Germans are observed with loathing. But the Germans are not the real target. What she is depicting is the grossness of the male, guzzling and drinking, pressing his unwanted attentions on the young girl in *At Lehmann's* and on the middle-aged wife in *Frau Brechenmacher Attends a Wedding*. Katherine Mansfield's own situation at the time, the pregnant girl surrounded by curious middle-aged matrons, is underlined in *Frau Fischer*. For all their German background and variety of characters, these stories are almost autobiography.

Back in London by early 1910 she found temporary refuge with Ida Baker, friend of her Queen's College days, who was to become her guardian angel thereafter. She placed her Bavarian stories with A. R. Orage's *The New Age* and shortly after embarked on a new love affair. The results were almost but not quite as disastrous as the first, and the young man faded from the picture. She began on more stories, some based on her Bavarian memories, two of them (*A Journey to Bruges* and *A Truthful Adventure*) springing from a brief visit to Belgium. *The New Age* published the latter two (they did not appear in book form until 1924) and a Bavarian story, *A Birthday*. These stories of 1911, though five of them are printed in *In a German Pension* (which appeared as a book late in 1911) show a mellower spirit than the 1910 stories. There is a certain genial and kindly humour in *The Advanced Lady*; and love, in *The Swing of the Pendulum*, in spite of the intrusion of a predatory male, leads to a conclusion acceptable to the central woman character. But nothing shows the change of attitude so clearly as *A Birthday*. The theme is the birth of a child, and the father, Andreas Binzer, is shown as (being a male, inevitably) selfish, but sensitive, nervous and finally overjoyed. There is nothing of the disgust with childbirth so clearly enunciated in *At Lehmann's* of the previous year.

What caused the change? Partly, one can only suspect, the happier love affair of this year. But there is a deeper reason. In *A Birthday*, Katherine Mansfield is for the first time drawing on her own family. In spite of the German names, *A Birthday* is set in Wellington, and Andreas Binzer is her first sighting-shot at the more than half true-to-life picture of her father which is to dominate so many of her later stories. In *A Birthday* there is a 'harbour', there are 'ferns' in a glass case, there is a 'gully', the wind shakes the window-sashes: the scene is New Zealand, Wellington so accurately depicted that one can to-day identify even the streets and the actual house in the story.

III

A few months after the publication of her first book, Katherine Mansfield moved on to her final love affair. This time, fortunately, it was permanent. The story of her meeting with John Middleton Murry in 1912 and their life together (they could not marry until 1918, when her husband divorced her) has been fully recorded by Murry and by Katherine Mansfield in her published letters. Henceforth, she had a centre to work from, and her early disastrous affairs, though they continue to provide a few themes for stories, sink below the horizon. But it is not mere gossip-mongering to record them. Without a knowledge of them the critic must read her early stories as mere literary exercises. They are more than that. They are a first beginning at the recording of experiences often little transmuted in the telling.

During the next two years Katherine Mansfield wrote stories for the two journals which Murry successively edited, *Rhythm* and *The Blue Review*. Most of these were based on New Zealand material. They fall into two groups. First, three tales of violence, all involving murder—the sort of thing that English readers readily associate with a rough colonial background. The best known of these is *The Woman at the Store*. The second group begins where *A Birthday* left off. The New Zealand 'Burnell' family begins to emerge, though they are not yet given a name: the little day-dreaming girl in *How Pearl Button was Kidnapped* (at first glance a mere fairy-tale), the bullying father, the tender grandmother, mother and the family of little girls, in *New Dresses* and *The Little Girl*.

Early 1914 saw the collapse of Murry's journals. During the year that followed, Katherine Mansfield wrote two of her best stories to date, *Something Childish, but very Natural*, a love-story which is evidently the Murry's love-in-a-cottage situation projected back to a couple of youngsters, and *An Indiscreet Journey*, based on a visit she paid to Paris in early 1915 to renew acquaintance with an old admirer. To these months also belongs *The Little Governess*, a longer story on several of her recurring themes—the young woman alone in the world, the predatory male, the unsympathetic foreign official. Katherine Mansfield had known them all. The story represents a technical advance. For the first time she is inside her character. We are at the beginning of that

sensitive feeling for characters portrayed through their own
fleeting thoughts which lies at the basis of all her mature
work.

IV

In 1915 occurred one of the several crises that determined
her life. Her brother arrived from New Zealand on his way
to the army. The exchange of old memories led to the
writing of two short New Zealand sketches, *The Apple Tree*[1]
and *The Wind Blows*. Before the end of the year the brother
was dead. When the first shock was over, she knew what
lay before her—the *recherche du temps perdu*: 'I want to write
recollections of my own country. Yes, I want to write
about my own country till I exhaust my store. Not only
because it is "a sacred debt" that I pay to my country
because my brother and I were born there, but also because
in my thoughts I range with him over all the remembered
places.'

She was ill, and the Murry's moved for a time to the
south of France. There at Bandol she completed in early
1916 her first major story, *The Aloe*, a recollection of New
Zealand. It was not published until 1930. She laid it aside
for revision. Emotion and nostalgia were not enough.
Technique required an intellectual effort that demanded
more time and cooler reflection. The revision was published
as *Prelude,* in 1918. It is the story that set the standard and
established the pattern for all her later work. The 'Burnell'
family are evoked in their early days, the little girls still
small children, Stanley Burnell at the opening of his pros-
perous career, the whole told 'in a kind of special prose'
(the phrase is her own) that is one of the secrets of her
originality.

During the two years following *The Aloe* she was increasingly oppressed by illness. She had seldom been
completely in health since her first arrival in London. By

---

[1] Among the stories and sketches which remain uncollected.

the end of 1917 her illness was diagnosed as tuberculosis and in early 1918 she was back in Bandol again. The year between the two visits to Bandol saw her returning on ten occasions to *The New Age*, but not with New Zealand stories. While *Prelude* was maturing in her mind as her major work, she was content to publish only lighter stuff, perceptive but not very deeply felt. *Mr. Reginald Peacock's Day* with its simpering hero, and *A Dill Pickle*, the story of the meeting of two disillusioned lovers, are typical of the group. The best of these is *Feuille d'Album*, an adolescent love-story, remarkable because it is her first full use of the interior monologue. In 1917 that meant being in the forefront of technical experiment.

Her writing of 1918 includes two New Zealand stories, *Sun and Moon*, on the surface an allegory but in fact a 'Burnell' family story of the *Prelude* group, and the unfinished *A Married Man's Story*, an 'interior' narrative in a Wellington setting. Her best two stories of the year are *Bliss*, with its innocently happy wife who recognizes in a moment of horrified insight her successful rival, and the polished *Je ne Parle pas Français*. This last represents a return to old experiences, handled with a technical competence which is approaching its peak. She revives her old memories of the woman on her own, abandoned in Europe by her lover. The situation of her earlier experience was reinforced by the circumstances in which she was writing. Murry was in London—where he had to earn a living. Katherine Mansfield, ill and alone in Bandol (except for the faithful Ida Baker), bombarding him with urgent and not always fair accusations of neglect, felt as abandoned as Mouse, who is finally deserted by her lover in Paris, in the caustic but effective ending of *Je ne Parle pas Français*.

By spring 1918 she was in London again. She was married to Murry in May. Illness prevented much writing, and in later 1918 it had to be the Continent again for the winter. *The Man Without a Temperament* with its theme of a sick wife and coldly patient husband is her comment on the period. It is of peculiar significance that its original title was *The Exile*. The summer was spent back in England. After arranging for the publication of a volume of her stories of the last few years—they were published as *Bliss, ond Other Stories* in late 1920, and included the subtle and evocative *Prelude*—she left again for the south of France. It was the final break with England, to which she was henceforth but a fleeting visitor. If she had to be an exile, it might as well be where her failing health had some expectations.

V

From then for a space of less than two years she worked with the concentrated fury of a woman who has only a little time to go. She had been publishing since she was nineteen. She was now thirty-two. The critics had ignored her first book in 1911. Her second, *Bliss*, was acclaimed on all sides. But she was dissatisfied with it: 'A great part of my Constable[1] book is *trivial*.' This is a harsh judgement. But in view of what she planned—and what she achieved in these remarkable two years—it was true.

The writing of these two final years was to yield a total almost as great as all the work of the remainder of her career. It was done in two bursts of fertile activity, the first at Mentone in the south of France during the winter of 1920-1, and the second from the middle of 1921 till the middle of 1922, when she was with her husband in Switzerland and later was undergoing treatment in Paris. The last half-year of her life (she died on 9 January 1923) understandably produced nothing that has survived.

At Mentone she wrote six stories. With her reputation rising rapidly, she found the solider literary journals were now waiting for her, and all six were published in *The Athenæum*, *The Nation*, and the *London Mercury*. Three are on her *leitmotiv* of the woman on her own in an unfriendly world. The central situations in *The Lady's Maid, Miss Brill*,

---

[1] Constable & Co. were Katherine Mansfield's publishers.

and *The Life of Ma Parker* are variations on this theme, with the lonely woman now slipping into middle-age. *The Daughters of the Late Colonel* is a magnificently envisaged story of two women devastated by the death of their father. In life he took everything from them, and his disappearance leaves them without a reason for existing. Constantia, the younger of the sisters, is observed from Ida Baker, who (the recently published *Letters* reveal) drove Katherine Mansfield to alternate fits of exasperation and gratitude. Both aspects are present in Constantia. *The Young Girl*, a slight but sensitive sketch of adolescence, and *The Stranger* complete the group written at Mentone. *The Stranger* is a New Zealand story. Stanley Burnell (what matter if he is now called John Hammond, who had been Andreas Binzer?) waits on the Auckland water-front for the liner bringing home his wife. Burnell is ageing, as so many of Katherine Mansfield's characters are at this time, but he is the same man, bustling in public, sensitive and vulnerable in his private relations. She has been delayed at the bedside of a dying passenger, and Burnell jealously resents the intrusion: 'They would never be alone together again.'

When she moved to Switzerland, the pressure of work mounted: 1921 was the busiest year of her life. Stories poured from her pen, finished and ready for the publishers, sometimes within an evening, though the themes had often been dormant for years. This is the great year of the 'Burnell' family sequence, lovingly remembered at various periods of their lives. *Sixpence* (excluded from *The Garden Party* volume of 1922 as 'sentimental') shows Burnell punishing his small boy and then relenting. The father-image has ceased being merely a big bully. In *An Ideal Family* he is sympathetically conceived (now 'old Mr. Neave') as an old, failing man, swamped by his three daughters and his son, who has taken over the business. In *Her First Ball*, daughter and son are young people, brought face to face with the cynicism of middle-age. *The Voyage* recounts an earlier memory, the heroine a mere child with her beloved grandmother. The series culminated towards the end of the year with the magnificent perception of *At the Bay*, where the children are youngsters at the family's seaside cottage, and *The Garden Party* (they are now the 'Sheridans'), where the girls and their brother are almost grown up, and they meet for the first time the horror of death—and life—on the other side of the street. Katherine Mansfield in these sensitively felt stories is not merely recording experience. She is expressing a view of life on a basis of recorded memories.

All of this group and the six Mentone stories were published in *The Garden Party and Other Stories*, early in 1922. They do not exhaust its contents. Along with some earlier work there was the love-story, *Mr. and Mrs. Dove*, delicately poised between mockery and sentiment, and a vicious delineation of a brittle woman rejecting the love of a devoted husband, *Marriage à la Mode*, written perhaps in contrition to make her peace with the writer of *The Man Without a Temperament*. *The Garden Party* evoked a chorus of praise on both sides of the Atlantic. By the end of the following year it had been reprinted once in England and seven times in America. If Katherine Mansfield wanted either popular fame or critical reputation, they both were hers now.

VI

It was too late to matter. Her illness was progressing, and she pushed ahead with her writing. Between the end of 1921 and the middle of 1922, when she ceased writing, she wrote sufficient stories for her final volume, *The Dove's Nest*, published in 1923 a few months after her death. It contains several stories on the relationship of husband and wife, *A Cup of Tea*, *Honeymoon*, *Widowed*, *All Serene!* and one on her recurring theme of the lonely woman, deserted even by her pet bird, *The Canary*. But the strength of the volume lies once again in the stories of her own town, pre-eminently in the classic re-creation of childhood, *The Doll's House*. The childhood is Katherine Mansfield's, the family is the now familiar 'Burnell' group, the scene is an authentic Wellington suburb, where the 'creek' and the house she describes are still discernible. But, like all her best New Zealand stories, it transcends mere locality. Her accurate rendering of background is only part of her larger accuracy in the rendering of life. To this final group of Wellington memories recalled belongs *Taking the Veil*, with its adolescent day-dreams, and, among the unfinished stories in the book, *A Bad Idea*, *A Man and his Dog* (which is an appendix to *Prelude*) and *Susannah*.

Two stories, both among the last things she wrote, bring the series to a close and complete the theme on which the death of her brother had launched her, the final repayment of the 'sacred debt'. The first is *Six Years After*—the title is self-explanatory for anyone with a knowledge of her life-history—where Stanley Burnell (he is now simply 'Daddy') and his wife start on a voyage. For him the bustle of shipboard is enough. For his wife the memory of the dead son makes the thought of the journey intolerable. *Six Years After* provides the clue to *The Fly*, which was assessed by that masterly critic of the short story, E. J. O'Brien, as one of the fifteen finest short stories ever written, 'as inevitable as the passage of time'. *The Fly*, written in early 1922, when she knew that the finish was not far off, is often asserted to be her 'indictment of life'. It is, rather, her clear-eyed admission that life goes on. Two old men, retired business man and boss (both, aspects of Burnell) linger over the memory of the boss's son, killed 'six years ago' in the war. When the old man goes, the boss plays with a fly ink-soaked on the blotting-paper, until the fly finally gives up the struggle:

> The boss lifted the corpse on the end of the paper-knife and flung it into the waste-paper basket. But such a grinding feeling of

wretchedness seized him that he felt positively frightened. He
started forward and pressed the bell for Macey.

'Bring me some fresh blotting paper', he said sternly, 'and look
sharp about it.' And while the old dog padded away he fell to
wondering what it was he had been thinking about before. What
was it? It was . . . He took out his handkerchief and passed it inside
his collar. For the life of him he could not remember.

This may be an indictment of life, but it is much more an
admission that the dead pass on, and the living must live
their own life. *The Fly* is full of symbolism that the author
may not herself have recognized. The spirit of the dead
brother, which had driven her on to such urgent activity,
was finally at rest. The debt was paid.

VII

Much of the above could not have been written in the
years immediately following her death, and criticism of
Katherine Mansfield has tended to fasten on what could be
judged solely from her published stories—her prose style,
her insight, her technique. All of these are important both
for an appreciation of her work and in view of the great
influence she had on the art of the short story. She had the
same kind of directive influence on the art of the short story
as Joyce had on the novel. After Joyce and Katherine
Mansfield neither the novel nor the short story can ever
be quite the same again. They beat a track to a higher point
from which others can scan a wider horizon.

Criticism of her published stories, however, is powerfully
reinforced and given a deeper significance by a knowledge
of the sources of her material. Such a knowledge has become
increasingly possible with the publications of Katherine
Mansfield's own 'background' writing—her *Journal* in
1927, her *Letters* in 1928, and more recently (in 1951) the
full text of her letters to her husband. The importance of
the New Zealand themes (for example) is clear enough to

any careful reader of her later stories. But when we turn to her *Journal* of that period and find her haunted night after night with dreams that she is on shipboard sailing back to her own country, we do not need to be psychoanalysts to see the connexion between *The Garden Party* and *The Doll's House* and the recurring dream-pattern.

Until quite recently Katherine Mansfield's *Journal* and *Letters* have been the best commentary on her stories. But they are sometimes fragmentary and leave unexplained considerable passages in her own history. Biographical studies, which should expand and supplement her own account, have been largely hampered by the 12,000-mile separation between the two parts of her life and also because so many of her associates are still alive and have been chary of discussion. Miss Ruth Mantz's study of 1933, although the author visited New Zealand, is slight, based on partial evidence, and leaves her subject with all her major stories still to write. Miss Sylvia Berkman's study of 1951 is a much more impressive piece of work, based on an accurate know-ledge of the printed materials, of which there was much more available than in 1933, but had the bad luck to be written and published before the full text of the letters was available. The most recent study (1953), by Mr. Antony Alpers, has made use of these letters, and overcomes both of the difficulties that biographers have encountered. A New Zealander with a substantial length of residence in England, he had thereby a considerable advantage in following the pattern of her development. In addition he was successful in persuading several people to give accounts, who had hitherto preserved silence, notably Miss Ida Baker and Mr. G. Bowden, Katherine Mansfield's first husband. Mr. Alper's biographical study is the fullest and most understanding written so far.

VIII

The material of Katherine Mansfield's stories, based so

directly on her own experiences, is in the central tradition of the English novel, the affairs of everyday heightened by sensitivity and good writing. Her range is even more restricted than Jane Austen's few families in a country village. For her, one family and a few relationships she had known were enough to express a universality of experience. Essentially the stress is on character and the subtle inter-relationships of people in small groups, bound together by bonds of emotion. To express these she concentrates her writing, discarding the heavy lumber of narration and descriptive backcloths. In the end she has not more than half a dozen themes. First there is the woman alone in the world, as she had been in her younger days. As Katherine Mansfield grows older, so does this character age, a girl in *The Tiredness of Rosabel*, a woman in *Miss Brill* and *Pictures*, an older defeated woman of *Life of Ma Parker* and *The Canary*. Secondly, there are the stories of the man and woman, for whom a happy relationship seems impossible, because the woman is the victim of a predatory or an in-different male, as in *The Little Governess*, *This Flower*, *The Man Without a Temperament* and *Je ne Parle pas Français*.

In a small group of stories, the situation is reversed. In *The Black Cap*, *The Escape*, and the bitter *Marriage à la Mode*, it is the husband who is loving and trusting and the wife who deserts him. Indeed, in Katherine Mansfield, a happy marriage relationship is only apparent in those stories which she based on her parents—'Stanley' and 'Linda', under these and other names, face life with confidence and together in the pages of *Prelude* and *At the Bay* and *The Garden Party* and can clearly survive the marital crises depicted in *The Stranger* and *Six Years After*.

Her other major theme is children in their relationships with one another and with the adults in the family. The child-father bond is subtly drawn in a series of magnificent studies, starting with the resentment of the young child against the omnipotence of the parent in *Sixpence*, *A Suburban Fairy Tale*, and *New Dresses*; through relief at his departure from the house and indifference towards him, expressed most clearly in *At the Bay*; to a recognition, in *The Little Girl*, that he is 'Poor father! Not so big, after all'; and finally to a growing sympathy for him and, as child and parent grow older, a recognition of his adult problems, in *An Ideal Family*. This sequence is rounded off with the warning conveyed in *The Daughters of the Late Colonel*, where the daughter-father bond has persisted till life without the parent becomes impossible.

All of these relationships may be found in other writers. But in the delineation of children together Katherine Mansfield stands alone. Her life-long discipline in entering into the mind of her subject ('I have just finished a story with a canary for a hero, and almost feel I have lived in a cage and pecked a piece of chickweed myself') is nowhere more essential than when the writer enters the mind of a child. If an adult writer portrays the mind of an adult character, only the most percipient critic can detect where the character is not fully realized and is 'contaminated' by the writer's own personality. Because of this, the delineation of adult character and the impact of adult on adult is, by comparison, easier. The writer may 'contaminate' his character with something of himself and still create on paper a credible personality. But the least 'contamination' by the adult writer's personality of the character of a child he is creating on paper shows up immediately. Few children are drawn in literature without some adult perception showing through. The author's feeling of adult condescension or regret for his own lost childhood usually comes over. The very titles of books like *The Golden Age* or *When We Were Very Young* imply an adult assessment. But Katherine Mansfield portrays children as children, seen through their own eyes and the eyes of other children. Kezia and Lottie and Isabel Burnell and the Trout boys Pip and Rags (and their dog, a uniquely children's dog) in *Prelude* and *At the Bay*, with the unforgettable Lil and Our Else in *The Doll's House*, are creations that stand by themselves in English writing.

IX

The technique of the stories of Katherine Mansfield's maturity lies partly in their construction and partly in her lyrical use of language. Straightforward chronological narration is seldom favoured, rather an alternation of time present and time past (and sometimes time future), with scenes juxtaposed to heighten the emotional effect. In *The Daughters of the Late Colonel* the two 'tenses' of the story (past, the happiness of life with father; present, the desolation of life without him) are implicit from the opening sentence, every apparently simple word of which has been written and placed with craftsmanlike care:

The week after was one of the busiest weeks of their lives.

The remainder of the story is an expansion of the implications of these opening words, in scenes alternating between present and past with occasional shuddering glances into the empty future. The story opens with the two women anxiously discussing the disposition of their dead father's effects; it slips back a few days (Nurse Andrews will stay on for a week as guest); a few days further back, to the death of Father; forward to the present—the visit of the clergyman; back to the past—the scene at the funeral; forward to the present, and the problem again of Father's things: should his watch go to their brother Benny or to Cyril, the grandson? The question has the effect of sending the story to the past again—a former visit by Cyril; and this merges into Cyril's visit to his grandfather, the old man presented not as a memory but living and grimly in action. The story finally returns (through an interior monologue by one of the sisters) and remains in the bleak present. This manner of presenting a story is familiar enough to-day. Virginia Woolf and Joyce, to name but two major figures, have made it a common-place in the novel. But *The Daughters of the Late Colonel* was written in 1920. *Ulysses* did not appear till 1922 and *Mrs. Dalloway* was published in 1925. Katherine Mansfield's handling of time and of interior monologue is her own.

Writing in her *Journal* of another story she is quite explicit about her method of construction:

> What I feel the story needs so particularly is a very subtle variation of 'tense' from the present to the past and back again—and softness, lightness, and the feeling that all is in bud, with a play of humour over the character.

This play of time backwards and forwards is done with great narrative skill. She discards the clumsy mechanism of scene-shifting of the typical novel of the nineteenth and the early twentieth century, and recaptures a narrative economy in transition from scene to scene that English fiction had lost since Jane Austen. In the story just mentioned, Cyril has written a note of condolence to his two aunts:

> Dear boy! What a blow his sweet, sympathetic little note had been! Of course, they quite understood; but it was most unfortunate.
> 'It would have been such a point having him', said Josephine.
> 'And he would have enjoyed it so', said Constantia, not thinking what she was saying.
> However, as soon as he got back he was coming to tea with his aunties. Cyril to tea was one of their rare treats.
> 'Now, Cyril, you mustn't be frightened of our cakes. Your Auntie Con and I bought them at Buzzard's this morning. We know what a man's appetite is. . . .'

This skilfully written passage starts in the present, glimpses to an unattainable future that is already past, shifts to the real future, and then, without a word of transition, introduces a long scene from the past.

The 'subtle variation of tense' is a notable feature of all her later stories. It is often used with peculiar appropriateness as one of her means of quietly unfolding character. In *At the Bay* and *Prelude* Stanley Burnell and his mother live in the bustling present, his wife Linda dreams in her steamer

chair beneath the manuka tree in a timeless past, Kezia and
the children occupy the eternal present of childhood, and
Beryl, the unmarried girl, lives in a continually imagined
future.

X

The second part of the passage quoted from her *Journal*
emphasizes the care with which Katherine Mansfield contrived the 'feeling' of each situation and character. Whether
her people are the little girls of *The Doll's House*, or school-
boys (like Hennie in *The Young Girl*), or selfish young men
and women (like the hero of *A Dill Pickle* or the heroine of
Revelations), or the older men and women of stories like
The Fly and *The Voyage*, the author never allows herself to
come on stage as a presenter of whose intrusion we are
conscious. She sinks herself inside each of her characters,
thinking or speaking in their tone of voice. *Prelude* opens
with the family disputing for space on the buggy:

> There was not an inch of room for Lottie and Kezia in the buggy.
> When Pat swung them on top of the luggage they wobbled; the
> grandmother's lap was full and Linda Burnell could not possibly
> have held a lump of a child on hers for any distance.

That 'lump of a child' is not Katherine Mansfield's comment. It is Linda's unexpressed thought, beautifully worked
into the structure of a sentence, which in its opening words
had the simple function of carrying the narrative and now
carries the tone of voice of one of the central characters.

This sense of always being inside the character is one of
Katherine Mansfield's greatest contributions to the craft of
fiction. Her interior monologues are, for contemporary
readers, readily recognizable, though there is nothing
mechanical or obvious about her use of them. In addition
to examples already mentioned, *The Little Governess*, *Feuille
d'Album*, *Taking the Veil*, and *The Doll's House* (to cite stories

both before and after she achieved her mature technique) all contain characters who are revealed through their own thoughts. But the 'innerness' of her character-drawing goes beyond the interior monologue. In her best stories the world is always seen through the eyes of one of her characters. Where she describes scenery, it is not merely the backcloth to a situation. It is conveyed to the reader emotionally, and uniquely, as only the person in the story can feel it. Episode VII of *At the Bay* is introduced by such a scene:

> Over there on the weed-hung rocks that looked at low tide like shaggy beasts come down to the water to drink, the sunlight seemed to spin like a silver coin dropped into each of the small rock pools. They danced, they quivered, and minute ripples laved the porous shores. Looking down, bending over, each pool was like a lake with pink and blue houses clustered on the shores; and oh! the vast mountainous country behind those houses—the ravines, the passes, the dangerous creeks and fearful tracks that led to the waters' edge.

The rocks like great beasts, the pool clustered round with 'houses' backed by mountains, the sense of fear and danger —this is not the confident and factual downward-looking view of the adult, it is the viewpoint of a small child seeing objects larger than herself, rendered even larger and more fearful by her fancy. The reader has in this manner been introduced to Kezia, the dreaming little girl, though he must read another full page before she appears in person. But she is there already. We have approached the beach through her eyes.

Subtler still is Katherine Mansfield's remarkable (one might even dare to say unique) ability to shift the point of view (and so introduce several characters) within the confines of a single sentence. The opening of *Prelude* has already shown a narrative sentence shaping itself into the colour of a person's thoughts. In *The Daughters of the Late Colonel* the two sisters ring for the maid:

> And proud young Kate, the enchanted princess, came in to see what the old tabbies wanted now.

Here within less than twenty words we shift from the point
of view of the two sisters, awed and obscurely envious of
the girl's dazzling youth, to the viewpoint of the maid,
haughtily resentful of her elderly mistresses having once
again rung the bell. Not a word need be added. Not a word
could be dropped. And yet it is all there.

XI

Several critics have pointed out the poetic qualities of
Katherine Mansfield's writing. The American critic, Conrad
Aiken, himself a poet, as early as 1921 in a review of *Bliss,
and Other Stories* made the essential point. Katherine
Mansfield writes the short story with the resources and the
intention of lyrical poetry. Her stories should not be (and
were not written to be) read as narratives in the ordinary
sense, although considerable narrative movement is implied
in the majority of them. She conveys, as a lyric poet conveys,
the feeling of human situations, and her stories have all the
unity and shapeliness and the concentrated diction of
implied emotion that characterizes the well-wrought lyric.
As with the lyric, her stories yield their full meaning only
on re-reading, when the reader can link up the implications
of phrase upon phrase that are not always apparent on the
first run-through. And like the lyrics of a poet the stories
illuminate each other. An early critic, G. S. Street, writing
in the *London Mercury* in 1921, confessed how he found his
clue to the apparently fragmentary *Bliss* when he re-read
the conclusion of *The Daughters of the Late Colonel*. This
illumination of one story by another is particularly evident
in the New Zealand family sequence, which, when read *as
a sequence*, not in the order of composition but in the inter-
nal time-order of the family's own history, is one of the
most sensitive and finely-conceived writings of our time.

Each separate part, even each separate phrase and word, of
her best stories contributes to the final emotional impression
of the whole. In *Mr. and Mrs. Dove*, the hero is young,

insecure, impressionable and romantic. How well this is captured in a few lines, as Reggie walks towards the house of the girl he is in love with:

> 'And where are you going, if your mother may ask?' asked the mater.
>
> It was over at last, but Reggie did not slow down until he was out of sight of the house and half-way to Colonel Proctor's. Then only he noticed what a top-hole afternoon it was. It had been raining all the morning, later summer rain, warm, heavy, quick, and now the sky was clear, except for a long tail of little clouds, like ducklings, sailing over the forest. There was just enough wind to shake the last drops off the trees; one warm star splashed on his hand. Ping! another drummed on his hat. The empty road gleamed, and the hedges smelt of briar, and how big and bright the hollyhocks glowed in the cottage gardens.

This is admirably done. It is not so much the articulation of the narrative as the implications of the words used that convey the impression of the very ordinary young man ('mater' and 'top-hole') who with a sense of release enjoys sensuously the sights and sounds and smells of the fresh afternoon. The fanciful duckling image, the sailing image, the 'gleam' of the road, and the 'one warm star splashed on his hand': the whole summer afternoon and his sense of elation are compressed into poetic language implicit with emotive overtones, the achievement of the aim she had, years earlier, set before her:

> Perhaps not in poetry. Nor perhaps in prose. Almost certainly in a kind of *special prose*.

One of Katherine Mansfield's greatest achievements lay in this, the creation of a prose style which could borrow from poetry, but which nevertheless remains prose, firmly based on a simple and even colloquial movement.

XII

Since the language—one might almost say the diction— of Katherine Mansfield's writing with its subtle evocation

of mood and scene and its poetical use of overtones is such
an important part of her meaning, it is important for the
English—or, for that matter, foreign—reader to remember
that certain of her words are used in a sense peculiar to New
Zealand, and not current in England. In her letters these
words and phrases are freely used. There she talks of
'swags' of strawberries; a good issue of a journal is 'a perfect
corker'; depressed by the winter weather of Italy she 'had
a rare tangi over this climate'; she will do better reviews
and send two 'bonzers'. 'Corker' and 'bonzer' are both New
Zealand slang words corresponding roughly to the current
English 'smasher'; 'swag' is the swagman's bundle; and
'tangi'—the word is Maori—is standard New Zealand
usage for a general lamentation.

In the stories also there is an occasional New Zealand
colloquialism, but only where it is appropriate, among the
small children, or on the lips of a workman:

> 'Say, cross my heart straight-dinkum.'
> The little girls said it.

★   ★   ★   ★

> But when they reached the top of the hill and began to go down
> the other side the harbour disappeared, and although they were
> still in the town they were quite lost. Other carts rattled past.
> Everybody knew the storeman.
> 'Night, Fred.'
> 'Night O', he shouted.

New Zealand words or usages of a more general nature are
introduced to evoke the local scene. The 'piece of loose
iron' that bangs on the roof in several stories should warn
the reader snug under slates or tiles that the early colonial
houses were roofed with corrugated iron, invariably referred
to simply as 'iron'. The 'creek' that runs through *Prelude* is
a little stream, not an arm of the sea. The 'bush-covered
hills' at the opening of *At the Bay* are covered with heavy
forest, not small bushes. Perhaps no word in Katherine

Mansfield, with her insistence on the importance of half-tones and 'quarter-tones', is so likely to convey the wrong tone as the 'paddocks' which surround the houses of her characters. 'Paddock' in English usage implies horses, with an undertone of hunting or at least pony club. Nothing could be further from Katherine Mansfield's meaning. 'Paddock' in New Zealand is simply the normal word for field—a grassy meadow into which Kezia and the children can run. On occasion the setting of the scene in New Zealand is done obliquely, without the use of local language, and yet with quiet precision. In *Prelude* towards the end of the day Kezia waits in the empty house:

> Kezia liked to stand so before the window. She liked the feeling of the cold shining glass against her hot palms, and she liked to watch the funny white tops that came on her fingers when she pressed them against the pane. As she stood there, the day flickered out and dark came.

This is not the close of an English day with its slow twilight and its imperceptible gradation to night. It is the quick oncoming of night that she remembered from the latitude of her childhood.

XIII

This essay has been confined to Katherine Mansfield's life-story, so far as it seems to be of importance for an understanding of her work, and a critical examination of the literary quality of her stories. There has been considerable writing on Katherine Mansfield (since the publication of her *Journal*) on her mysticism, her 'secret', her isolated 'purity', which would make her a vaguely symbolic and saintly figure. It cannot be denied that chapter and verse can be found for much of this kind of thing in the later entries in her *Journal*. It is well to remember that in her final year she was a very sick woman, facing death with only the rags of a Christian faith and ready to grasp at dubious 'philo-

sophic' alternatives; she was, too, throughout her whole
life in many ways (though never in her craft) naïve. She
had the intellectual gaps of the self-educated woman that
she was. The final scenes of faith-healing under the guidance
of a crazy Russian while she formulated a spiritual creed
can hardly be the basis for a fair judgement either of her
real quality or of her view of life. Katherine Mansfield the
writer had laid down her pen many months before that
melancholy final passage.

There is nothing vague or nebulous—or naïve—about
her writings. She is assured in her craft, and knowledgeable
even to the placing of a comma. She writes with precision,
knowing the effect she intends, and achieving it in all her
best work with an accuracy and an inexplicable rightness
in prose expression that is perhaps in the end the only real
secret that died with her. And without ceasing to belong
to the country that bred her, she is one of the few writers
so far who have in any worthy way repaid something of
the debt that the Commonwealth owes to the literature of
England.

XIV

POSTSCRIPT

The disparity between the assured professionalism of the
short stories and the other-worldliness that emerges from
the *Journal* is something that I have always found difficult to
reconcile. Yet there, published in the *Journal* of 1927 and
the expanded definitive edition of 1954, were her own
comments on life and letters, clearly a primary—if not
indeed *the* primary—source for both biographer and critic.
It was up to each to effect his own reconciliation of the two
Katherine Mansfield's, or even (as I attempted some years
ago in the previous section, which I have deliberately left
unaltered) to ignore the wraith of the *Journal* and focus
attention on the meticulous craft of the story-teller.

There the matter might have had to rest. But the death, in 1957, of John Middleton Murry brought on the market a large collection of her notebooks and manuscripts. These were bought by the New Zealand Government for the Alexander Turnbull Library, Wellington. They consist of four diaries (for 1914, 1915, 1920, and 1922), which (like most other people's diaries) peter out somewhere between February and March, some thirty notebooks filled with story fragments, ideas for stories varying from a few words to several pages, quotations, personal observations, notes on her reading, lists of household expenses kept in meticulous detail, accurately kept income and expenditure accounts (she was very much, as it appears, the banker's daughter), and some hundred single sheets on to which are copied poems, 'vignettes', a chapter of her abortive novel *Maata*, an unfinished play, and some finished stories copied out ready for the printer. It is a remarkable record of a writer at work.

A close comparison of this heterogeneous mass of material with the books published after her death has revealed some interesting facts. From this untidy heap of material Murry created the *Journal* of 1927; from some of the left-over pieces he created the *Scrapbook* of 1939; and working over it once again a decade later he created the 'definitive' *Journal* of 1954. Murry was a brilliant editor. His most brilliant work was the synthesis of his wife's loose papers in what became—justifiably—recognized as a minor classic.

But synthesis it was. Katherine Mansfield did not keep a 'journal' in any usual sense of the word. She bought occasionally a pocket diary and for a few weeks made brief entries. In her working notebooks, among the drafts of stories and notes on possible situations and characters, she made from time to time a personal entry or observation. Something like half of the published *Journal* consists of passages that were in no recognized sense 'journal' material; indeed one or two of them are demonstrably story-frag-ments, fiction not personal records. The editor has interpolated these pieces, often at precise dates, even where his own pencilled notes on the source material reveal that he has doubts about the date. He regularly salvages passages of poetry (by herself and others) which she had copied out—sometimes on a single undateable sheet—and inserts them at 'appropriate' places, to expand and illuminate a diary entry which originally stood in isolation. Occasionally a passage from one notebook is run together without indication, with a passage from another notebook of different date. The omissions, even in the 'definitive' edition, are considerable. The working writer, the business woman—the banker's daughter—drop out of sight. There is nothing in the published versions of the *Journal* that is not by Katherine Mansfield. But by selection and by manœuvring the raw material, particularly by the juxtaposition of passages originally unconnected and by printing diary entries continuous with scraps of story drafting without indication of the change in his material, the editor has created something that was not in the manuscripts and notebooks, a *persona*, an idealised picture of his dead wife.

It is a curious business so to dismember a book that many readers have come to cherish. And one must be fair. Murry is absolutely scrupulous in his own pencilled annotations on the Mansfield manuscripts. He indicates his omissions, and sometimes even writes in his reasons for the omission. He handled the actual documents like a scholar. He published what he decided to transcribe as a creative editor. He was, after all, writing a memorial portrait, not a biography.

But whatever the literary value of the published *Journal*, its value to biographers and critics is severely limited by the editorial method. Any further biographical or critical work on Katherine Mansfield will have to be based on the notebooks and not on the *Journal*, which no longer can retain the status of a primary document. The Katherine Mansfield of the *Journal* is an intense and over-rarefied spirit, conjured up by piety and affection. From the notebooks, as a full edition will show, she emerges as what must be a truer and certainly a more interesting figure, the writer in the workshop with her nose to the grindstone. There was, as one had always suspected, only one Katherine Mansfield. She is not as pleasant a creature as the *persona*. She is more business-like, ruthless on occasion, and sometimes quite cold-blooded. But she is a much more credible human being.

KATHERINE MANSFIELD

Select Bibliography

BIBLIOGRAPHY

MANTZ, RUTH E. *The Critical Bibliography of Katherine Mansfield*. London: Constable, 1931.

There is also a long list of critical and biographical studies in Sylvia Berkman's *Katherine Mansfield*, 1951 (see below); this work also corrects some inaccuracies in Ruth Mantz's bibliography.

COLLECTED EDITION

Collected Stories. London: Constable, 1945.

SOME SELECTIONS

Stories. Selected with an Introduction by Elizabeth Bowen. New York: Vintage Books, 1956.

Selected Stories. Edited by D. M. Davin. The World's Classics. London and New York: Oxford University Press, 1953.

The editor is a New Zealand scholar and novelist.

SEPARATE WORKS

Listed in the order of first publication. Place, publisher, and date of the first American edition (if any) follow the entry on the British edition.

In a German Pension. London: Stephen Swift, 1911; New York: Knopf, 1926. *Stories*.

Katherine Mansfield refused to allow this volume to be reprinted in her lifetime.

Prelude. Richmond, Surrey: Hogarth, 1918. *Story*.

Handprinted by Leonard and Virginia Woolf at the original Hogarth Press.

Je Ne Parle Pas Français. Hampstead: Heron Press, 1919. *Story*.

Published (and stitched and bound) by John Middleton Murry and his brother for private circulation.

Bliss and Other Stories. London: Constable, 1920; New York: Knopf, 1921. *Stories*.

The Garden Party and Other Stories. London: Constable, 1922; New York: Knopf, 1922. *Stories*.

The Dove's Nest and Other Stories. London: Constable, 1923; New York: Knopf, 1923. *Stories*.
Published posthumously, and edited with an introductory note by John Middleton Murry, as were the following items.

Poems. London: Constable, 1923; New York: Knopf, 1924. *Verse*.

Something Childish and Other Stories. London: Constable, 1924; New York: Knopf, 1924. *Stories*.
The U. S. A. edition is entitled *The Little Girl*.

Journal of Katherine Mansfield. Edited by John Middleton Murry. London: Constable, 1927; New York: Knopf, 1927. *Autobiography*.
A fuller, but not definitive edition, also edited by Murry, was published in 1954 (London: Constable).

GORKY, MAXIM. *Reminiscences of Leonard Andreyev*. Translated by Katherine Mansfield and S. S. Koteliansky. London: Dulau, 1928; New York: Random House, 1928.

The Letters of Katherine Mansfield. Edited by John Middleton Murry. 2 vols. London: Constable, 1928; New York: Knopf, 1929.
A much fuller edition, entitled *Katherine Mansfield's Letters to John Middleton Murry, 1913–1922,* also edited by Murry, was published in 1951 (London: Constable; New York: Knopf). The earlier edition contains some items omitted from the later edition.

The Aloe. London: Constable, 1930; New York: Knopf, 1930. *Story*.
Includes the original form of *Prelude, 1918.*

Novels and Novelists. Edited by J. Middleton Murry. London: Constable, 1930: New York: Knopf, 1930. *Criticism*.
Beacon Press Paperback.
Reprints in their entirety Katherine Mansfield's reviews of fiction contributed from April, 1919 to December, 1920 to *The Athenæum*.

Poem: To Stanislaw Wyspianski. London: Priv. Ptd., 1938. *Verse*.
Privately printed for Bertram Rota, from a MS of 1910, and not edited by John Middleton Murry.

The Scrapbook of Katherine Mansfield. Edited by John Middleton Murry. London: Constable, 1939; New York: Knopf, 1940. *Miscellany*.

BIOGRAPHICAL AND CRITICAL STUDIES

SULLIVAN, J. W. N. "The Story-Writing Genius," *The Athenæum* (April, 1920).

AIKEN, CONRAD. "The Short Story as Poetry," *The Freeman*, Vol. III (May, 1921).

ARMSTRONG, MARTIN. "The Art of Katherine Mansfield," *The Fortnightly Review*, Vol. CXIII (N.S.) (March, 1923).

HUBBELL, GEORGE S. "Katherine Mansfield and Kezia," *The Sewanee Review*, Vol. XXXV (1927).

WAGENKNECHT, EDWARD. "Katherine Mansfield," *The English Journal*, Vol. XVII (1928).

MANTZ, RUTH E., AND JOHN MIDDLETON MURRY. *The Life of Katherine Mansfield*. London: Constable, 1931.
Almost entirely on her early years. Inadequate and superseded by Sylvia Berkman's *Katherine Mansfield* (see below) and Antony Alpers' *Katherine Mansfield* (see below).

CARCO, FRANCIS. *Souvenirs sur Katherine Mansfield*. Paris: Librairie Le Divan, 1934.
Recollections by a writer whom Katherine Mansfield used in several of her French stories.

SCHNEIDER, ELIZABETH. "Katherine Mansfield and Chekhov," *Modern Language Notes*, Vol. L (1935).

MAUROIS, ANDRÉ. *Prophets and Poets*. New York: Harper, 1935.

SEWELL, ARTHUR. *Katherine Mansfield: A Critical Essay*. Auckland, N. Z.: Unicorn Press, 1936.

CATHER, WILLA. *Not Under Forty*. New York: Knopf, 1936.

MURRY, JOHN MIDDLETON. *An Autobiography: Between Two Worlds*. New York: Messner, 1936.

BEAUCHAMP, SIR HAROLD. *Reminiscences and Recollections*. New Plymouth, N. Z.: T. Avery, 1937.
Contains a chapter on Katherine Mansfield by G. H. Scholfield.

ORTON, WILLIAM. *The Last Romantic*. New York: Farrar and Rinehart, 1937.

BATES, HERBERT E. *The Modern Short Story*. New York: Thomas Nelson, 1941.

GORDON, IAN A. *Katherine Mansfield, New Zealander*. N. Z. New Writing. Wellington, N. Z.: Progressive Publ. Soc., 1943.

PRITCHETT, V. S. "Books in General," *New Statesman and Nation,* Vol. XXXI (N.S.) (February, 1946).
Review of *Collected Stories.*

"Katherine Mansfield's Stories," *The Times Literary Supplement* (March, 1946).

LAWLOR, PATRICK A. *The Mystery of Maata: A Katherine Mansfield Novel.* Wellington, N. Z.: Beltane Book Bureau, 1946.

MURRY, JOHN MIDDLETON. *Katherine Mansfield and Other Literary Portraits.* New York: British Book Centre, 1949.

BERKMAN, SYLVIA. *Katherine Mansfield: A Critical Study.* New Haven: Yale University Press, 1951.
Contains a detailed life, mainly from printed sources, but supplemented by information from Katherine Mansfield's sister. An excellent study.

ALPERS, ANTONY. *Katherine Mansfield: A Biography.* New York: Knopf, 1953.
The most detailed and complete biography, from sources previously available, supplemented by much new material gathered from Katherine Mansfield's associates.

WRIGHT, CELESTE T. "Katherine Mansfield's Father Image," *University of California Publications, English Studies* No. 11 (1955).

WALKER, WARREN S. "The Unresolved Conflict in 'The Garden Party,' " *Modern Fiction Studies,* Vol. III (1957).

MURRY, JOHN MIDDLETON. *Katherine Mansfield and Other Literary Studies.* London: Constable, 1959.
Contains Murry's fullest appreciation of Katherine Mansfield in print. Not the same as his *Katherine Mansfield and Other Literary Portraits,* 1949.

GORDAN, IAN A. "The Editing of Katherine Mansfield's Journal and Scrapbook," *Landfall* (Christchurch, N. Z., March, 1959).

BATESON, F. W., AND B. SHAHEVITCH. "Katherine Mansfield's 'The Fly': A Critical Exercise," *Essays in Criticism,* Vol. XII (1962).

GENERAL CRITICAL STUDIES OF
E. M. FORSTER, VIRGINIA WOOLF
AND KATHERINE MANSFIELD

Select Bibliography

MUIR, EDWIN. *Transition: Essays on Contemporary Literature*. New York: Viking, 1926.

DOBRÉE, BONAMY. *The Lamp and the Lute: Studies in Six Modern Authors*. Oxford: Clarendon Press, 1929.

VERSCHOYLE, DEREK, ed. *The English Novelists*. New York: Harcourt, Brace, 1936.

HOARE, DOROTHY. *Some Studies in the Modern Novel*. London: Chatto and Windus, 1938.

DAICHES, DAVID. *The Novel in the Modern World*. Chicago: University of Chicago Press, 1940.

RILLO, LILA E. *Katherine Mansfield and Virginia Woolf*. English Pamphlet Series No. 17. Buenos Aires: Argentine Association of English Culture, 1944.

CECIL, LORD DAVID. *Poets and Story-Tellers*. New York: Macmillan, 1949. Contains an essay on Virginia Woolf and E. M. Forster.

SAVAGE, DEREK S. *The Withered Branch*. New York: Pellegrini and Cudahay, 1952.

JOHNSTONE, JOHN K. *The Bloomsbury Group*. New York: Noonday Press, 1954.
A study of E. M. Forster, Lytton Strachey, Virginia Woolf, and their world.

EDEL, LEON. *The Psychological Novel 1900–1950*. Philadelphia: Lippincot, 1955.

DAICHES, DAVID. *The Present Age in British Literature*. Bloomington: Indiana University Press, 1958.
Introductory survey, with bibliographies.

KARL, FREDERICK, AND M. MAGALANER. *A Reader's Guide to Great Twen-tieth-Century English Novels.* New York: The Noonday Press, 1959.
Conrad, Forster, Virgina Woolf, Lawrence, James Joyce, and Aldous Huxley.

SCHORER, MARK, ed. *Modern British Fiction.* Galaxy Book. New York: Oxford University Press, 1961.
Essays on Forster, Woolf, Lawrence, Joyce, Hardy, Conrad, and Ford Madox Ford.

COX, C. B. *The Free Spirit: A Study of Liberal Humanism in the Novels of George Eliot, Henry James, E. M. Forster, Virginia Woolf, and Angus Wilson.* London: Oxford University Press, 1963.

Virginia Woolf writes about Katherine Mansfield in *Granite and Rainbow,* and about E. M. Forster in *The Death of the Moth.* Katherine Mansfield reviews books by Virginia Woolf and by E. M. Forster in *Novels and Novelists.* E. M. Forster writes about Virginia Woolf in *Abinger Harvest;* he also chose to devote to her his Rede Lecture at Cambridge (published as *Virginia Woolf*).

Further studies are listed in: the Annual Bibliographies published in *PMLA* by the Modern Language Association of America; *The Year's Work in English Studies,* a survey of important critical books and articles, published annually for the English Association by the Oxford University Press; the *Annual Bibliography of English Language and Literature,* an extensive listing of critical books and articles, published for the Modern Humanities Research Association by the Cambridge University Press; and the Current Bibliographies, annotated lists of articles about contemporary writers, published in each issue of the quarterly journal *Twentieth Century Literature.*